Do-It-Yourself Decorating
Step-By-Step
Wallpapering

Julian Cassell & Peter Parham

Meredith® Press

Des Moines, Iowa

Contents

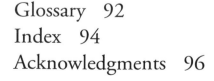

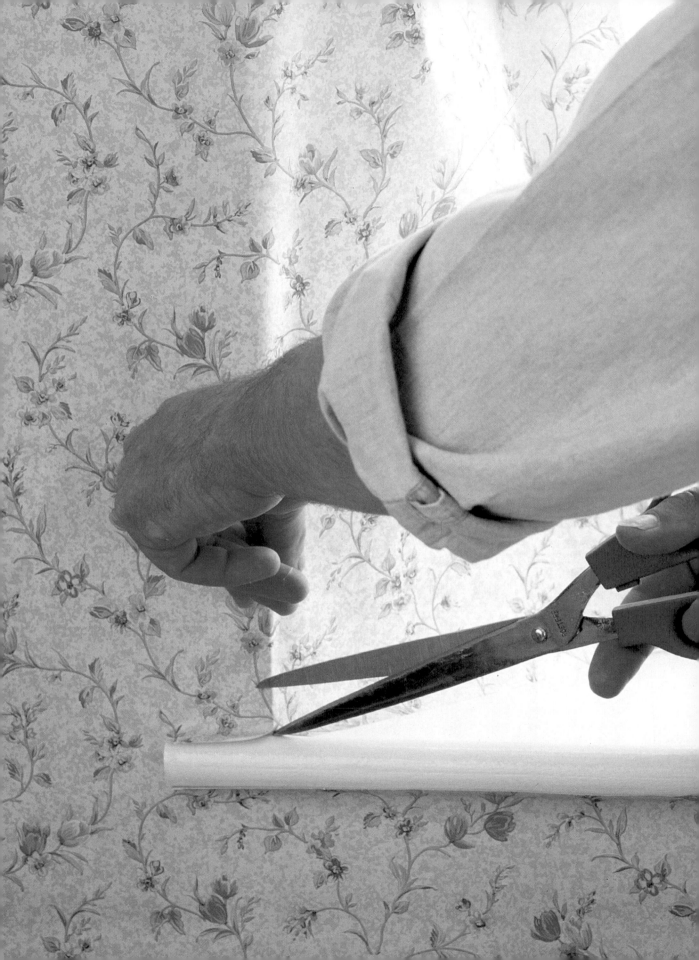

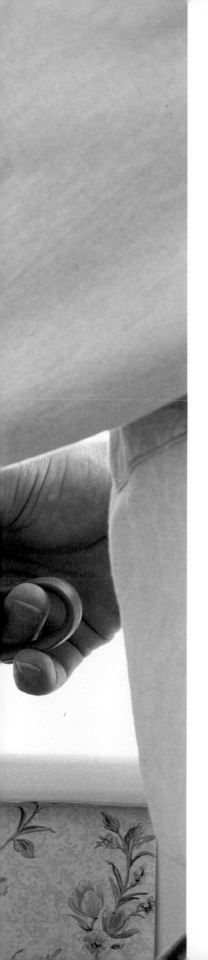

Introduction

Wallpaper can work dramatic and surprisingly speedy transformations on your rooms. And today's wallpaper palette has more colors, patterns, and textures than ever before. If you take time to shop around, you'll find everything from bold colors to soft ones and from geometric patterns to classic florals. If you want something more subtle, you'll appreciate the simply elegant textures of tone-on-tone stripes, softly dappled "sponged" looks, and rich relief designs that mimic the intricate patterns found in centuries-old plaster.

Hanging wallpaper is easier than ever, too. Start with "Ideas and Choices" (page 6) for a gallery of decorating options and practical pointers on choosing the right paper for each room.

Just as with painting, preparation is everything. "Planning and Preparation" (page 16) starts by showing you all of the tools and materials you may need, then takes you step-by-step through patching and preparing your surfaces. The "Lining" chapter (page 30) reveals more tricks of the trade for achieving professional results.

The largest chapter, "Wallpapering" (page 50), covers every facet of hanging paper, including determining the best place to start, learning how to handle tricky joints and corners, and fixing common mistakes and problems. Even if you've wallpapered before, you'll find new ways to speed your work and get professional-looking results.

Ideas and Choices

Deciding on a color or pattern may be the most difficult part of wallpapering, especially if you're trying to match the paper to a particular color of paint, furnishings, or carpet. Take advantage of the advice you may get from interior designers and design reference books, but also pay attention to your own instincts. If a design is pleasing to your eye—and if you keep coming back to it after looking at alternative coverings—it's probably right.

This chapter will show you the visual effects that are possible with various types of wall coverings. It also will give you valuable guidelines on the all-important practical aspects of paper and help you choose the right kind of paper for each room.

As you make your design decisions, don't hesitate to collect swatches of your favorite colors and fabrics, clip pictures from magazines, and borrow lots of paper sample books. They'll all help you choose a wallpaper that offers a color and pattern to please you for years to come.

Color schemes and designs

We've all seen how color can affect our mood, and the dominant color of wallpaper is no exception. Warm colors such as oranges and yellows "advance" to create a welcoming atmosphere. Cooler colors such as greens and blues can give the impression of space and set a fresh, soothing mood. When a wallpaper design contains several colors, it can be hard to decide which one is dominant. In that case, it's often the boldest or darkest color that predominates.

Pattern size is just as important as color. Large patterns are more dramatic, but smaller, busier patterns are better at hiding surface imperfections and often are more forgiving of small pattern-matching mistakes. Symmetrical patterns such as stripes are perhaps the most challenging to hang—and also the most revealing of any surface irregularities.

◀ Large floral designs are classic decorative wallpaper patterns. Always take into account room size when you're using them because they can overpower a small area. In rooms meant for relaxing, large floral patterns like this will help you create a feeling of luxury and elegance.

◄ Smaller, repetitive designs create a more active impression. They also help to hide imperfections in the wall and minimize mistakes in pattern matching. They make excellent backdrops for paintings, ornaments, and architectural features such as wainscoting.

► Wallpaper should complement the other colors in a room. Choose your woodwork paint colors carefully, and always make a test patch of the paper and paint before you buy enough to do an entire room. (Hint: If you're unsure of your paint color, buy just a quart of paint and roll it on part of the wall. Then, check its effect with your wallpaper sample in both daylight and lamplight.) When you're happy with the color scheme, consider combining your wall covering with decorative painting effects such as the faux marbling on the panels shown here.

Creating a mood

Choose your wallpaper carefully and you can change the look and "feel" of any room. For example, a lattice pattern lends casual, porchlike ambience to a basic sitting room; a small dotlike pattern on a white background gives a small room an airy country feeling; and a dark, richly hued covering wraps a large room in newfound intimacy. Also consider how you'll use the room most often, the style and vintage of your home, and the backdrop that the paper will create for the room's furnishings.

Finally, remember that you'll use different rooms more at certain times of the day. Make sure you compare wallpaper samples under both natural and artificial lighting to be sure that the colors are exactly what you want.

◄ In a bedroom or other private spot, you have lots of room for exploring your personal decorating tastes. Here, a bold yet classic plaid turns a small and once-dull room into a casual country retreat. Note how the wall covering and windows work together to form a unit: The wallpaper design mimics the larger grid of the windows, which are painted to match the dusty blue in the wall covering.

▶ Borders are another decorative option and can produce stunning effects when they divide two different types of wallpaper. Many papers are designed to be painted over, such as the embossed paper below this chair rail.

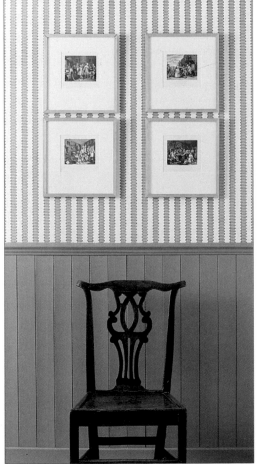

◀ Striped papers always create a sense of order, often with a traditional feel. They're especially effective used alongside a complementary patterned paper or with a matching paint color on wainscoting. Such vertical lines visually raise a low ceiling.

Practical papering

When you select wallpaper, it's important to consider the practicality of the paper for the room it's decorating. Some wallpapers are especially delicate and shouldn't be used in areas that get hard wear. The different paper "finishes" are explained and illustrated on pages 14–15, but the examples on these two pages offer suggestions on ideal areas of use for wall coverings with different properties.

◄ Any material you put in a bathroom must be able to withstand the harsh effects of condensation and moisture. In such locations, a vinyl covering is ideal because its washable—or sometimes even scrubbable—coating protects it and keeps it easy to clean. Today, practical vinyl wall coverings are available in a range of handsome colors and patterns.

◀ Children's rooms can be great fun to decorate because they let you experiment with bold colors and patterns. As well as being decorative, borders neatly divide the walls into upper and lower sections. Not only can a border rescale a tall ceiling and bring the focus down to a child's level, but it also can draw a line between a decorative pattern above and a more durable paint treatment below. Since children tend to subject the lower sections to more wear and tear, consider using a washable semigloss or gloss paint on the wall area below the border.

▼ The kitchen is another area that needs constant cleaning. Relief papers, which suggest designs that craftsmen once worked in plaster, produce a durable surface that you can paint in bold colors to enhance their texture or treat with softer tones for classical elegance. Again, a border complements the wallpaper design.

Wallpaper finishes

Wall coverings come in different finishes to suit various purposes. Some are especially hard-wearing; others are purely decorative.

The most common types of wallpaper are shown here, but there are still other papers available that have slightly different characteristics. Always be sure to read the manufacturer's directions before buying these papers so they'll be right for your intended use.

Lining

Flat, plain paper sometimes hung on bare wall surfaces as a smooth base for decorative wallpaper.

Standard pattern

Flat wallpaper with a design machine-printed onto its surface.

Natural textures

Whether made of smooth fabric, such as wool or felt, or nubbier linen, burlap, or grasscloth, these heavy wall coverings serve two functions. They enrich any room with warm texture while serving as beautiful disguises for rough or damaged wall surfaces.

BORDERS

Decorative borders are available in various finishes. Typically applied horizontally at ceiling or chair-rail level, they also are used to outline and emphasize special architectural features.

WALLPAPER SYMBOLS

Check the label symbols for characteristics such as washability, hanging method, and pattern match.

Vinyl

Popular, mass-produced vinyl papers come in a wide variety of patterns. A clear vinyl layer is bonded on top of a printed pattern. They're easy to keep clean and ideal in areas that require frequent washing, such as kitchens and bathrooms.

Heavy-duty vinyl

Thick, hard-wearing vinyl papers are particularly good in damp areas such as kitchens and bathrooms that need constant cleaning. Because they're so much heavier than standard wallpaper, they need a strong adhesive or they're likely to peel off the wall.

Expanded vinyl

Made by only a couple of U.S. companies today, expanded vinyl has a textured finish created by air injected into it at the liquid stage during manufacturing. The textured design tends to be more hard-wearing than that on embossed papers (see below).

Hand-printed

There are two main types of hand-printed papers: screen-printed and block-printed. Both are printed one roll at a time. Pattern matching can be difficult, and edges may need trimming before hanging. Usually pricey, this paper also is stunning.

Embossed

A relief pattern is imprinted in the paper during manufacturing, producing a raised decorative surface. Plain white papers usually are painted once they're hung, but others have a printed pattern. Be careful not to flatten the relief during application.

Flocked

Flocked papers are patterned with fibers embedded in the surface. Originally they were made from silk or wool, but today they are more commonly made from synthetics, which are easier to hang. The pattern is mounted on flat backing paper.

Planning and Preparation

For successful wallpapering results, careful planning and preparation are essential. For the job to go properly, you'll need to make important decisions about the necessary materials, tools, and steps involved in your project. All wall coverings, regardless of price or quality, need a sound and well-prepared surface on which to hang, so the hard work involved in preparation is just as important as the actual paper hanging. Work carefully now, and you can count on professional results that last.

Tools

When choosing and buying tools and equipment, always opt for quality over quantity. A few carefully selected quality tools will serve you better than many cheaper ones.

As you shop for tools, don't feel you need to buy everything you see here. Instead, buy just for your specific needs and accumulate your tools gradually. Also, if you'll use an item only occasionally, especially if it's an expensive one such as a steam stripper, it may be more economical in the long run to rent it.

BASIC PREPARATION TOOLS

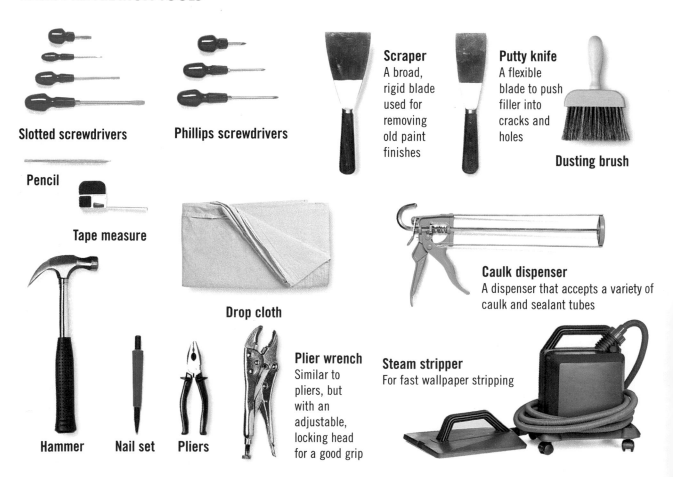

Slotted screwdrivers

Phillips screwdrivers

Scraper
A broad, rigid blade used for removing old paint finishes

Putty knife
A flexible blade to push filler into cracks and holes

Dusting brush

Pencil

Tape measure

Drop cloth

Caulk dispenser
A dispenser that accepts a variety of caulk and sealant tubes

Hammer

Nail set

Pliers

Plier wrench
Similar to pliers, but with an adjustable, locking head for a good grip

Steam stripper
For fast wallpaper stripping

Access and working surfaces

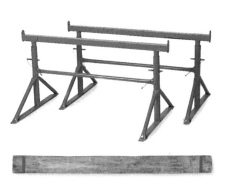

Sawhorses and boards
For a sturdy platform when working
on ceilings or high walls

Stepladder

Pasting table

Personal protection

Protective gloves
Waterproof, to protect
hands from chemicals

Goggles
Keep dust, spray, and
chemicals out of eyes

Dust masks
(disposable)

WALLPAPERING TOOLS

Paper-hanging scissors

Crafts knife

**Crafts knife with
snap-off blades**

Stirring stick

Bucket

Sponge

Measuring cup

Wallpaper trough

Level

Steel rule

Chalk line
Marks a long,
straight line where
the distance is too
long for a steel rule

Plumb line
Determines a
true vertical

Seam roller
Presses
joints flat
when
hanging
paper

Brush
For pasting edges

Pasting brush

Roller

Paper-hanging brush

Identifying problems

Before starting your surface preparation, clear the room. It's best to remove all furniture, accessories, and soft furnishings and to take up rugs and protect carpeting now. If it's not possible to totally clear the room, move everything to the center and protect it with drop cloths. Now you can get a clear view of any problem areas and decide how to fix them.

If you'll need to do any painting, it's best to do it before you hang the wallpaper. As a general rule of thumb, you should start by preparing all surfaces, line ceilings and walls if necessary, do any painting, and finally hang your wallpaper. It's a lot easier to wipe excess paste off a painted surface than it is to clean paint spatters off an expensive wall covering.

The problems shown here are ones you should look for and correct before you start to wallpaper.

DAMPNESS AND MOLD

Mold is caused by a buildup of moisture, normally due to poor ventilation. Wash the area with a fungicide. Extensive mold growth may require professional treatment, and if there's an underlying dampness problem, it should be corrected before wallpapering. Old moisture stains should be covered with a commercial sealer.

CRACKS IN PLASTER

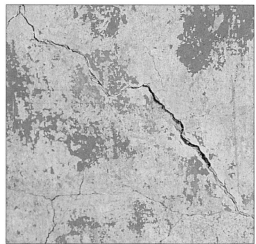

Cracks can be caused by walls that have dried out, by the structure settling, and by general wear and tear. Use an all-purpose filler to fill them and allow them to dry completely before papering the wall (see pages 26–27).

POWDERY WALL SURFACES

Found in older houses previously painted with water-base paint; also caused by the breakdown of plaster due to age. Before papering, wash and seal (see pages 28–29).

EFFLORESCENCE

This fluffy, grainy texture found on both old and new walls results from the crystallization of salts in the building materials. Scrape away the deposits until no more appear.

FLAKY PAINT

Caused by moisture under the paint or by paint that couldn't stick to a powdery or an incompatible surface (see Dampness and Mold, page 20, and Powdery Wall Surfaces, left).

FLAKING TEXTURED FINISHES

Caused by water penetration (such as a leaking pipe) or a poorly prepared wall surface. You'll need to remove all textured finishes before starting to wallpaper.

UNEVEN PAPERED SURFACES

Generally found in older homes. If the paper is basically sound or a "rustic" look is acceptable, don't strip the old paper; the plaster underneath may come off with the paper.

WRINKLED LINING PAPER

Common in corners where the walls aren't square or where settling has lifted and torn the paper. Cut out small areas with a scraper and fill them with fresh liner before papering.

BUBBLING PAPER

Bubbles almost always are caused by sloppy papering or poor adhesion to the wall. Strip all the paper (see pages 24–25) before hanging lining paper and a new wall covering.

LIFTING SEAMS

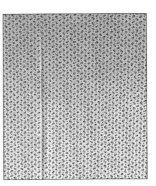

Caused by poor paste adhesion. Reglue small areas of lining paper with seam adhesive before papering. Lifted seams on wallpaper usually require stripping and repapering.

Paper and materials

Wallpaper is the most expensive item on your shopping list, so be careful when calculating the number of rolls you'll need. But you'll need more than paper to do the job right, so scan the supplies shown here as a visual checklist to round up what you'll need for the paper you've chosen.

As with tools, remember that poor-quality materials may slow your work. The best products may cost more, but it's usually money well spent.

BASIC SUPPLIES
Fillers

All-purpose filler
For holes and cracks

Premixed filler

Flexible filler
For joints and cracks where movement is likely

Stripping, sanding, and sizing

Sanding block
Sandpaper already attached to a supporting block

Stripper
For stripping wallpaper

All-purpose cleaner
Cleans walls prior to painting

Sandpaper
Fine, medium, and coarse grits

Spray-on stain block

Primer/sealer
For sealing surfaces before painting or papering

Size
Makes walls less absorbent and papering easier

Crafts-knife blades
Replace often to keep a sharp edge

Drop cloth

Paper hanging

Seam adhesive
Stronger than regular paste

Wallpaper paste

Premixed paste

Border adhesive

PAPERS

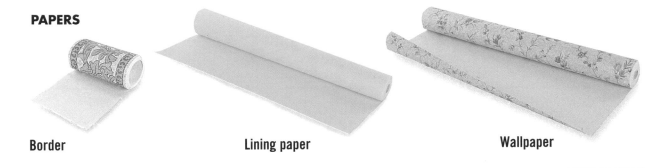

Border   **Lining paper**   **Wallpaper**

MEASURING

First, think about pattern repeats (see page 54). Papers with a large repeat pattern tend to produce more waste than those with a small repeat pattern.

To find out how many rolls of wallpaper you'll need, calculate the total area to be papered: See the diagram at right, which shows the easiest method.

1 Measure these two lengths and multiply them to calculate the area of the ceiling.

2 Measure these two lengths and multiply them to calculate the area of the wall to the right of the fireplace. Use the same technique to calculate the area of all other walls. Don't deduct anything for obstructions such as doors and windows, because you'll need to compensate for waste that occurs when you trim and apply the paper.

3 For wallpapering with patterned paper, allow for the unavoidable waste by adding the size of the repeat pattern to the height of the room when you calculate the surface area.

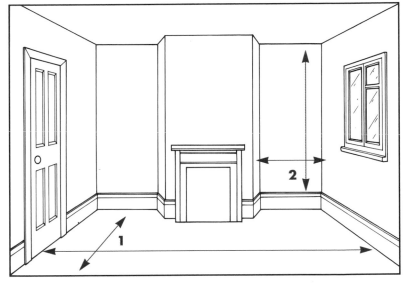

ROLLS OF WALLPAPER NEEDED

Total Surface Area to Paper	No. of Rolls	
sq. yd.		
6	1	For every additional
12	2	6 square yards, add
18	3	1 roll of wallpaper.

A standard roll of wallpaper is approximately 20½ inches× 11 yards = 6¼ square yards. The extra ¼ square yard per roll allows for trimming and waste.

If you're not using standard rolls, simply determine the surface area of the rolls you're using and create your own table like the one above.

Stripping paper

This is a time-consuming job, but if you follow these steps, it's reasonably straightforward. A steam stripper, which you can rent, speeds the work. When using it, always wear rubber gloves and goggles, as boiling water and steam can spit out from the sides of the stripping pad. If a steam stripper isn't available, soak the paper with hot water or use a wallpaper stripper. You'll still need gloves and goggles because most stripping chemicals irritate the skin.

TOOLS: Gloves, goggles, steam stripper, scraper, liquid measuring cup, bucket, stirring stick, 5-inch brush, wallpaper perforator

MATERIALS: Liquid stripper concentrate, hot water

STEAM-STRIPPING

1 When using a steam stripper, always read the instructions. Check that the steam stripper is turned off at its power source, then pour water into its reservoir. (Warm water will reduce the time needed for the stripper to boil.) Then switch on the power and wait for the water to boil. Never leave a steam stripper unattended when it's switched on.

2 Put on your goggles and gloves for protection. Then, place the stripper's steam pad firmly on the wall covering, holding the pad in the same position, without moving, for about 30 seconds. Some heavy papers may require a longer steaming time.

3 Move the pad across the wall and use a scraper to strip off the loose, bubbling paper. Avoid digging the end of the scraper into the wall, gouging holes in the plaster. You'll soon develop a rhythm of stripping the paper with one hand while you steam the next section with the other.

STRIPPING WITH WATER

  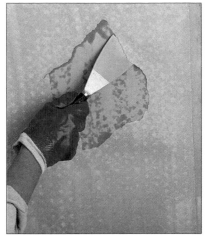

1 Measure hot water into a bucket and add the amount of stripper per manufacturer's instructions. Stir thoroughly until the stripper is completely dissolved. Hot water alone also works for soaking wallpaper.

2 Using a large brush, apply the solution to the paper, working from the top down. Don't soak more than a few square yards at a time or the paper will dry out before you have a chance to strip it off.

3 Let the paper soak for a few minutes, then strip it with a scraper. It's a good idea to clean up as you go or the stripped paper will dry out on your drop cloths and may be difficult to remove later on.

STRIPPING VINYL WALLPAPER

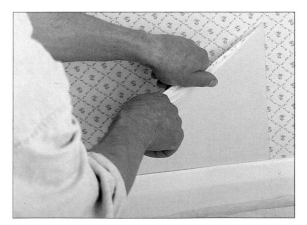

With vinyl papers, it may be possible to pull the top layer away from the backing paper without using a spiker or scorer. Don't leave the backing paper on the wall even if it's in good condition. It's not a suitable surface for wallpapering.

IDEAL TOOLS

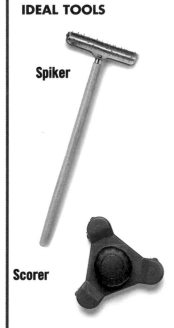

Spiker

Scorer

With all types of wallpaper, it's a good idea to break the surface before applying the stripper solution. There are several different types of tools you can use. They often are called perforators, spikers, or scorers, but all work the same way: They penetrate the paper, letting water and stripper in underneath to speed removal.

Patch ceilings and walls

Cracks and holes in walls and ceilings are common problems caused by slight settling in the structure or just everyday wear and tear. To repair them, use a commercially available filler or patching compound. Flexible fillers are best for areas of potential movement, such as cracks around door trim. Convenient premixed fillers come ready to use, but powdered fillers that you mix with water let you prepare just the amount you need.

TOOLS: Putty knife, dusting brush, 1-inch paintbrush, broad knife, sanding block, hammer

MATERIALS: Premixed filler or powdered filler and water, fine-grade sandpaper, newspaper, lumber, nails

1 Use the edge of a clean putty knife or a scraper to carefully clean out the area that's damaged. Brush out any loose debris before filling.

2 If you are not using premixed filler, pour the amount of powdered filler you need onto a clean surface. A plastic bucket lid is ideal for this purpose. Refer to the manufacturer's instructions for how much filler to mix at one time. Gradually add water, mixing the filler to a creamy but firm consistency.

3 Dampen the hole and the area around the hole with water. This lengthens the drying time so the filler is less likely to shrink. It also helps the filler bond.

IDEAL TOOL

When patching an old wall that has many small cracks, a broad knife will cover a large area quickly. Use it just like a putty knife. It's also excellent for patching wide holes because its large blade can rest on the edges around the hole, keeping the filler level as you work.

4 Load some filler on the putty knife and draw it across the hole, using the flexibility of the knife to firmly press the filler into the hole. You may need to draw the knife across the hole two or three times to cover the area completely and to make sure the filler is firmly in place. Always try to fill the hole slightly higher than the surrounding area to allow for a small amount of shrinkage. When the hole is filled, use the knife to clean any excess filler from the wall around the hole. This will minimize the amount of sanding you'll have to do when the filler dries.

5 When the filler is dry, sand the area with fine-grit sandpaper. Then run your fingers over the hole to make sure it's smooth and flush with the rest of the wall. If you find irregularities, dust off the area, wet it again, and reapply a thin coat of filler to any indentations that remain. Deep holes can be difficult to fill with just one application of filler. Bulging will occur where the filler isn't able to bond with the surrounding area of the wall. In such cases, use several thin coats of filler to gradually fill the indentation until it's level with the surrounding wall surfaces.

FILLING DEEP CRACKS

Sometimes it's necessary to fill a large, deep crack, such as in the corner of a room. Before filling, wad up a sheet of newspaper and, using a putty knife, press it firmly into the crack. This will give the filler a base to sit on while it dries.

FILLING A CORNER

To repair an outside corner, start by nailing a thin length of lumber flush to one edge of the corner. Fill the hole using a putty knife or other broad knife. When the filler has dried thoroughly, sand the area, remove the lumber, then repeat the process on the adjacent corner edge. Finally, fill the four nail holes you made when you tacked on the lumber. This will restore the original square corner edge.

Cleaning and sealing

Before hanging lining paper or wallpaper, clean and seal the walls and ceiling. Wall coverings applied to unstable or dirty surfaces may look good at first, but they will eventually deteriorate. Although these all-important first steps cannot be seen when your work is complete, you'll find that they add to the quality and longevity of the finish, and ensure that your work will pay off in years of beauty.

TOOLS: Bucket, sponge, 1½- and 4-inch paintbrushes, gloves

MATERIALS: Sealant/oil-base undercoat, aerosol stain block, size/ wallpaper paste, all-purpose cleaner, primer/sealer, water

SEALING

1 Water stains are common but respond to proper treatment. Consult a professional if an area remains wet; you may have an exterior problem that needs attention. If the stain is old and dry or the problem has been corrected, apply a commercial sealant or an oil-base undercoat to the area.

2 Some nondescript stains keep reappearing despite using a sealant. Commercial aerosol stain blocks will take care of most marks that are difficult to cover.

3 For new plaster, first apply a coat of sizing or diluted wallpaper paste. Either will seal the surface for good paper adhesion and even absorption. Either also will let you more easily slide the paper on the wall to match seams and patterns.

CLEANING

1 Prepare ceilings and walls to be papered by cleaning them with commercial wall cleaner or mild detergent solution. Mix the cleaner with warm water according to the manufacturer's instructions.

2 Wear protective gloves when using commercial cleaners, which may irritate the skin. Make sure you clean all surfaces thoroughly to ensure proper adhesion of your wall covering later on. When the surface is clean, rinse with clean water and a sponge. Let the area dry completely before continuing.

4 A primer or sealer is ideal for sealing porous or dusty surfaces because it bonds the wall surface together and acts as a smoothing undercoat before you begin papering. Because products vary, be sure to follow the manufacturer's instructions.

5 Apply the primer or sealer liberally for good coverage. Brush in any drips or runs that occur. When the area is dry, run your hand over the surface to make sure that it's no longer dusty or powdery. If it is, apply a second coat.

PAPERING OVER GLOSS PAINT
On surfaces that have been painted with gloss paint, sand the painted surfaces to roughen them and provide tooth for the paper.

SIZING EACH SURFACE
As well as sizing bare wall surfaces before hanging lining paper, remember to size lining paper before hanging the wallpaper itself. This makes it easier to position the paper on the wall.

Lining

Whether you are eventually going to paint or wallpaper a room, using lining paper on walls and ceilings makes all the difference in getting a professional rather than an amateur finish. Lining paper smooths out wall imperfections and provides an ideal surface on which to decorate.

A commonly held belief says that you must line horizontally before wallpapering and vertically for painting purposes. The choice is a purely practical one, however: The aim is to cover the ceiling and/or walls with the fewest number of lengths in order to make the best use of your time and effort.

This chapter will show you how to approach lining a room using the correct techniques and how to overcome any problems you may encounter.

Preparation

Before hanging lining paper, decide how many rolls you'll need to complete the job. Use a tape measure and the table opposite to make your estimate.

The diagram on page 23 shows the best way to calculate surface areas. There's no right or wrong place to start; just treat each area separately. Mentally divide your room into different areas as shown opposite and determine the best direction to line; this also will help you plan your order of work. Begin with the ceiling; it's easier than most walls because there are fewer obstructions to work around.

When you line a wall horizontally, start at the top and work down. Working from the bottom up may cause problems when you seam the paper higher up, especially after papering around an obstruction such as a doorway, window, or fireplace.

TOOLS: Tape measure, pocket calculator, pencil and paper, 2 buckets, liquid measuring cup, stirring stick

MATERIALS: Wallpaper paste, water

1 When you set up your equipment, stay organized. Put buckets of paste and clean water under the table to save space and to avoid accidents. Always keep your table clean and uncluttered. Try to keep everything you need close at hand to save time and energy.

2 When mixing up paste, make sure your equipment is clean. Always read the manufacturer's instructions; they can vary with different brands of paste. Measure the right amount of cold water using a liquid measuring cup.

3 Start to stir the water, then sprinkle the powder slowly into the bucket. Continue to stir for 2 minutes after adding all the paste. Let it stand for another 3 minutes, then stir again to make sure there are no lumps. It's now ready to use.

USING A PLATFORM

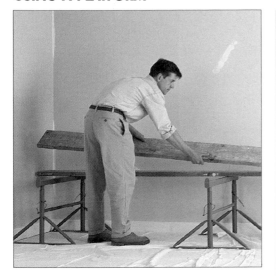

It's important to work on a safe, solid platform—especially when papering a ceiling. Sawhorses are excellent supports, but two stepladders with a sturdy board are a good compromise. Always use extra support under the middle of the board if you're spanning a large area.

MEASURING

Follow steps 1 and 2 on page 23, and calculate the amount of lining paper you need from the table below. There's no need to allow extra for pattern repeat when using lining paper.

ROLLS OF LINING PAPER NEEDED

Total Surface Area to Line		No. of Rolls	
sq. m.	sq. yd.		
5	6	1	For every additional
10	12	2	6 square yards, add
15	18	3	1 roll of lining paper.

A standard roll of lining paper is 22 inches×11 yards = 6¾ square yards. The extra ¾ square yard per roll allows for trimming and waste.

If you're not using standard rolls, simply determine the surface area of your rolls and create your own table like the one above.

Order of work

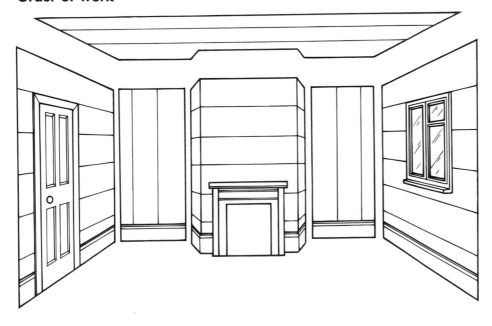

DOUBLE-LINING

On particularly uneven walls, you may need to hang two layers of lining paper before hanging the wallpaper. Make sure the seams on the second layer don't fall on top of those on the first.

Cutting and pasting

When cutting lengths of lining paper, always add 4 inches to your base measurement to allow for a 2-inch overlap at each end for final trimming.

    After pasting, allow about five minutes for the paste to soak into the paper. This makes it less likely to bubble, more pliable, and easier to work with. Once you start work, write a number on each length: You may have three or four soaking at once, and this will help you keep them in the right order.

TOOLS: Pasting table, tape measure, pencil, steel rule, scissors, pasting brush, paper-hanging brush, sponge

MATERIALS: Lining paper, wallpaper paste, water

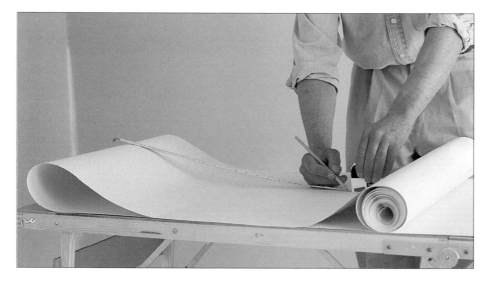

1 Carefully unroll the lining paper along the length of your worktable. If you need long pieces of paper, gently fold the paper back on itself along the table. Use a tape measure to determine the length of paper you need. Then make a pencil mark in the center of the roll where you'll need to cut.

2 Keep the edges of the paper flush with the edges of the table. This will help you make a square cut. Line up a straightedge at the pencil mark, check that it's square, and draw a line along its length.

3 Cut a straight line along the pencil mark. Then lay the paper flat on the table with the excess falling over one end. Use the paper-hanging brush to anchor the other end of the paper.

4 Line up the paper flush with the edges of the table to avoid getting paste on the face of the paper. Apply the paste evenly, working from the center out and covering the whole area.

5 When the paper on the table is pasted, gently fold the pasted end over, starting a bundle. Pull the bundle to one end of the table, again using the paper-hanging brush to hold the other end.

6 Continue to apply the wallpaper paste to the remaining lining paper, working up to the end of the table. Always make sure that the paste is applied in even strokes so it covers all areas of the paper. Try to avoid getting any paste on the face of the paper.

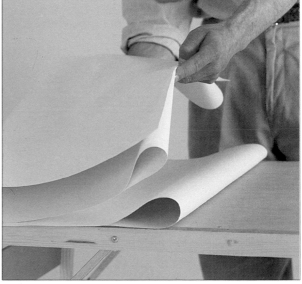

7 Keep folding the paper back on itself in a bundle. When you've pasted the entire length of the paper, remove it from the table and let it soak for the required time (per manufacturer's instructions). Wipe the table off with a damp sponge to clean up any excess paste.

Ceilings

Always try to line ceilings by working across the long dimension of the room so you can do it with fewer lengths and save a little time. Make sure you have a solid platform on which to work. Sawhorses spanned with boards work well because they let you get close to the ceiling line at both ends of the platform. Try to work so the top of your head is 9 to 12 inches from the ceiling.

Lining a ceiling isn't as difficult as it may appear. After you hang the first length and establish a straight edge, the other lengths go much quicker.

TOOLS: Sawhorses and boards, paper-hanging brush, pencil, scissors, small brush for pasting edges, sponge

MATERIALS: Lining paper, wallpaper paste, water

1 Arrange the work platform under the area where you want to start. Carefully lay the bundle of paper on the platform, and pick up one end.

2 Start papering at the edge of the ceiling. Keep the paper edge parallel to the adjacent wall. Using the paper-hanging brush, push the paper into the junction, allowing for a 2-inch overlap.

3 When the paper is securely pasted at one end, move slowly along the platform, brushing the paper from the center out in a herringbone motion. Keep the edge of the paper close to the wall to use it as a guide. Brush the paper in place, and repeat Step 2 at the opposite end.

4 When the length is hung, run a pencil along the wall-ceiling junction in a straight line. Or, use the blade of a pair of scissors to make a crease.

EASIER CEILINGS
Papering a ceiling is easier and less tiring with two people. One can hold the paper while the other maneuvers it into place.

5 Carefully peel back the paper. Using the paper-hanging scissors, cut a straight edge along the pencil line or scissors crease.

6 Push the paper back into position. Work along the length, checking for bubbles and lifting seams at the edges. Apply extra paste wherever needed.

7 After each length is hung, immediately wipe any excess paste from all surfaces so it won't leave a stain.

Hang the next length in the same way, placing its edge against that of the first. Slide the paper into position to make a neat butt joint.

Walk down the platform, brushing out the paper and making sure the seam is tight along the entire length. Trim the paper at each end as before.

DEALING WITH GAPS
If the wall isn't square, you'll notice one or more gaps along the wall-ceiling junction. You probably can fill a small gap (see page 43). But if a large gap appears, just move the paper closer to the wall, creating a longer overlap. Then simply trim this overlap as shown in steps 4–6 above.

Ceiling fixtures

Most ceilings have at least one light fixture that you'll have to paper around. Two methods work well. The first, shown in steps 1–5, is to pull the hanging fixture's cord through a cut in the paper. The second and often better method, shown in the box on page 39, is to measure the distance from the starting wall to the ceiling fixture so you can plan to have the cord fall on a seam between two lengths.

TOOLS: Sawhorses and boards, paper-hanging brush, scissors, crafts knife, small brush for pasting edges, sponge, screwdriver

MATERIALS: Lining paper, wallpaper paste, water, clean cloth

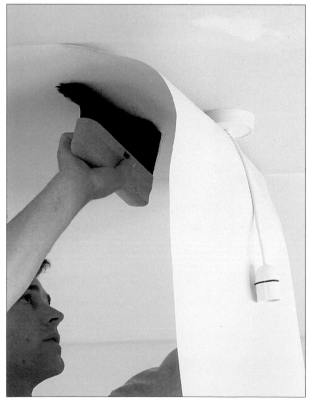

1 Don't try to make cutouts for ceiling fixtures ahead of time. Instead, when you reach the ceiling fixture with a length of pasted paper, gently brush the paper against the fixture so you can see exactly where to cut around it.

ELECTRICAL SAFETY
Always remember to turn off the power before starting to work around any lighting fixture, wall switch, or wall outlet.

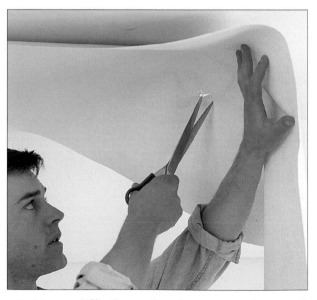

2 It's not difficult to tailor the paper to fit around ceiling fixtures. Support the loose side of the pasted paper with one hand. Using scissors, carefully mark the center of the fixture on the underside of the paper and make a small cut.

3 If there is a hanging cord, gently pull it through the cut, being careful not to tear the paper. Then brush out the rest of the paper, continuing to the wall on the other side of the room.

4 Using a pair of scissors, make a series of small cuts out to the edge of the ceiling fixture. Work all the way around it, but be careful to avoid cutting beyond the edges.

5 Crease around the edges of the fixture and trim the paper with a crafts knife. Brush out any remaining bubbles and wipe excess paste from the cord using a dry cloth.

METHOD 2: SEAM JOINT

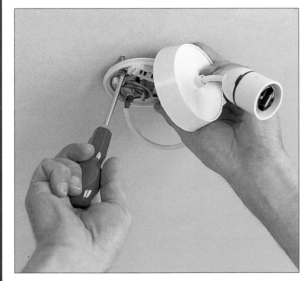

1 Always turn off the power at the electrical box. Remove the fixture's cover and loosen the retaining screws. Then let the entire fixture drop a couple of inches.

2 Using the paper-hanging brush, tuck the paper edges under the fixture's base. Reattach the base with the retaining screws and then replace the fixture cover.

Walls

You can hang lining paper on walls horizontally or vertically. Choose whichever direction is easiest. Vertical lining works well for small alcoves because fewer lengths are needed. A long wall is covered much quicker with horizontal lengths. For vertical lining, use a corner as your starting point; to hang lining paper horizontally, start at the line where the wall and ceiling meet.

Because horizontal lengths usually are longer than vertical lengths, you'll have larger bundles when you fold your pasted paper. Make your folds shorter so you end up with a smaller bundle that's easier to manage with one hand.

TOOLS: Sawhorses and boards, paper-hanging brush, pencil, scissors, crafts knife, small brush for pasting edges, sponge

MATERIALS: Lining paper, wallpaper paste, water

HORIZONTAL LINING

1 Start papering at the top of the wall, leaving a 2-inch overlap around the corner onto the adjacent wall. Line up the top edge of the paper with the junction of the wall and ceiling. If the junction isn't square, move the paper so it overlaps the ceiling and trim as usual when you've hung the entire length of paper.

2 Slowly release the folds of the pasted paper bundle, smoothing the paper along the wall with a paper-hanging brush. Brushing from the center of the paper out, continue to the other corner of the room. Keep the top edge of the paper flush with the junction of the wall and ceiling.

3 Make a pencil line at the corner or crease the corner with scissors, then gently pull the paper away from the wall. Trim the excess with scissors or a crafts knife.

4 Use the brush to push the paper back into the corner. You may need to add some paste if the edge of the paper has dried out during trimming. Repeat Steps 3 and 4 at the other end.

CROOKED ROOMS

If the wall or ceiling is especially crooked (and you've had to overlap the lining paper onto the ceiling), you won't be able to use the wall-ceiling line as a guide for hanging the entire length. To avoid hanging the first length at an angle, hold a level at the bottom edge to make sure it's perfectly straight. If the walls aren't square and you can't use a corner as your guide when lining vertically, use your level to establish a straight line.

VERTICAL LINING

1 Vertical lining works especially well around obstructions like exposed pipes. Start the first length flush with the pipes and push the paper behind them to hide the joint.

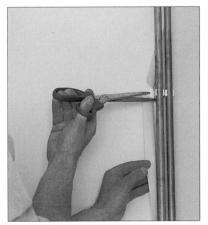

2 Mark the locations of any brackets or clips with a pencil, and then make two small cuts to their edges. Push the paper around the brackets and trim the excess paper.

3 Cut another length of pasted paper and use it to create a butt joint with the previous one. Smooth and trim the paper as before, pushing the paper's edges behind the pipes; wipe excess paste off the pipes.

Corners

When lining walls, the only corners you need to paper around are outside corners—those that protrude into a room. It's usually easier to start and stop the paper at inside corners; trying to paper around them causes bubbles and adhesion problems. Then go over the corner with a flexible sealant or filler to finish the seam. Don't try to paper around an outside corner that's not square; instead, make an overlapping butt joint, as shown opposite.

TOOLS: Sawhorses and boards, paper-hanging brush, scissors, steel rule, crafts knife, sponge

MATERIALS: Lining paper, wallpaper paste, water, sealant or filler, powdered filler, sandpaper, cloth

EXTERNAL CORNERS

1 Approach the outside corner holding the horizontal bundle of pasted paper in one hand. Use the other hand to push the paper to the corner, keeping its horizontal edge against the ceiling or the edge of the paper above it to make a neat butt joint.

2 Fold the paper around the corner using the paper-hanging brush to eliminate any bubbles under the surface. Make sure that the top edge of the paper doesn't overlap the paper above it.

3 Run your fingers gently along the corner to check for any wrinkles or creases in the paper. Smooth them out, if necessary. Then hang the rest of the length of paper, eliminating bubbles as you work.

UNEVEN OUTSIDE CORNERS

 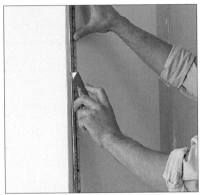 

1 For an uneven corner, bend the horizontal length around the corner and trim off all but a 2-inch overlap. Do this with each (horizontal) length on the corner. Then hang the next length (around the corner) vertically on top of the overlaps.

2 On the wall with the vertical length, line up a straightedge 1¼ inches from the corner. Using a crafts knife, cut a straight line down the straightedge. Then move the straightedge and continue cutting all the way to the baseboard.

3 Pull back the paper and gently remove the excess (overlapping) strips. Push the paper back into position with the paper-hanging brush. Finally, clean the area with a damp sponge to remove any excess wallpaper paste.

INSIDE CORNERS

1 We recommend trimming all lengths at an inside corner because this creates a neater joint. Run a bead of sealant or flexible filler down the corner and along the top of the baseboard.

2 Smooth the filler with a wet finger. This also will prevent the edges of the paper from lifting up later. Finally, wipe up any excess filler with a clean, damp cloth.

FILLING GAPS

Small gaps between lengths are sometimes unavoidable. Fill them with patching compound then sand them smooth.

Doors and obstructions

Some built-in room features—such as the trim around fireplaces and doors—stick out from the wall and require you to cut lining paper to fit around them. Regardless of the obstruction, the paper-hanging technique is the same. It simply involves careful trimming of the paper into angles and along edges, as we've demonstrated here with a fireplace and an interior door.

TOOLS: Sawhorses and boards, paper-hanging brush, pencil, scissors, crafts knife, small brush for pasting edges, sponge

MATERIALS: Lining paper, wallpaper paste, water

FIREPLACES

1 When the paper reaches the fireplace, let it flop over the top corner of the mantelpiece. Next, make a cut diagonally toward the upper part of the corner, being careful not to let the paper below tear under its own weight.

2 After making this initial cut, ignore the paper fold on top of the fireplace for now. With the paper-hanging brush and scissors, push the paper gently into the angles of the mantelpiece, making small right-angle cuts to let it lie flat on the wall.

3 Trim the small flaps with a crafts knife, getting as close as possible to the molding and leaving no gaps. Continue to paper along the top of the mantelpiece and repeat steps 1–3 at the other corner. Then trim the fold on top of the mantelpiece.

4 Messes are inevitable but easily taken care of. Clean any excess wallpaper paste off of ornate woodwork right away to prevent staining. Use a clean, damp sponge, and be sure to get all the paste out of cracks and molding.

DOORS

2 With both hands now free, you'll be able to feel for the corner of the door trim. Cut diagonally toward this point with scissors. Carefully pull back the excess paper over the door. Using the paper-hanging brush, firmly push the paper on the wall above the door into the edge of the trim until it is snug. Do the same at the other corner.

3 Using a crafts knife, trim away the excess paper, working carefully around the side and top edges of the door trim. Wipe excess paste as needed.

1 Allow the length of pasted paper to fall over the corner of the door trim. Continue hanging the rest of the length, loosely pasting it to the wall as you go.

Recessed windows

The technique for lining around a recessed window combines a number of steps already covered in this chapter. Here, you need to heed the order in which you hang the lengths of paper in order to produce the best possible finish. The method shown here also comes in handy for lining around recessed doors and alcoves.

TOOLS: Sawhorses and boards, paper-hanging brush, scissors, crafts knife, brush for pasting edges, steel rule, sponge

MATERIALS: Lining paper, wallpaper paste, water

1 Hang the first length of paper horizontally, as usual, letting the pasted paper extend right across the recess. When you have the paper neatly butted against the previous length of paper, return to the window and make two vertical cuts about ⅝ inch in from the corners of the recess. Carefully continue these cuts right up to the top edge of the window recess.

2 Starting in the middle, use the paper-hanging brush to push the flap of paper you've made back into the recess, working out any air bubbles as you go. Move the brush along the edge, continuing the process until the paper is in place on the ceiling of the recess.

3 Make sure the paper is secure in the junction between the window frame and the upper part of the recess before trimming as usual.

4 Fold the ⅝-inch flap around the corner of the vertical recess, using your brush and fingers to smooth away any air bubbles. Add more paste to the edge of the paper if it has started to dry too quickly. Hang the next length of paper, again allowing a flap about ⅝ inch wide to fold around into the recess. Repeat this step at the opposite side of the window recess.

5 Depending on the height of the window recess, you may need to hang more lengths of paper before reaching the windowsill. At the sill, carefully trim the paper using a series of right-angle cuts to fit the paper around the corner of the windowsill and underneath it. When you've completed one side, repeat this step at the opposite corner of the windowsill.

6 Measure and cut a panel of paper to line each vertical return of the recess. Line straight edge of the paper with the vertical corner, covering trimmed overlaps of the previous lengths.

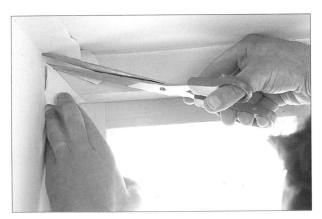

7 Make diagonal cuts into the top corner of the recess. Repeat at the bottom corner to help with final trimming. Fill any small gaps as shown on page 43.

REFINING YOUR TECHNIQUE

Unfortunately, this method of overlapping different pieces of lining paper doesn't always leave you with a perfectly flat surface. The small cuts that you have made around the vertical outside corners of the window recess can cause lumps in the paper that you paste over the top. If that happens, don't worry. Curtains probably will cover any imperfections. Or, as you become more skilled at paper-hanging, you may want to try your hand at making overlapping butt joints for neater-looking outside corners (see page 43).

Wall switches and outlets

Light switches and electrical outlets are common features of walls, but, fortunately, they do not pose insurmountable obstacles. It might seem difficult to paper around them, but you'll find that the job requires more time and patience than artistry. It's especially important to do a neat job with wall switches because you'll look at them every time you enter or leave a room. Whatever their size or shape, the steps are the same.

Always remember to turn off the power at your electrical box before working near any electrical switch or outlet.

TOOLS: Paper-hanging brush, pencil, scissors, screwdriver, crafts knife, small brush for pasting edges, sponge

MATERIALS: Lining paper, wallpaper paste, water, dry cloth

1 Turn off the power at the electrical box. Paper directly over the top of the switch or outlet, creating a butt joint as usual.

2 Brush gently over the light switch or electrical outlet, letting it form an impression in the paper. Be careful not to tear the paper as you work.

3 Holding the paper firmly over the switch or outlet, use a pencil to make small diagonal marks ¼ inch in from each of the corners.

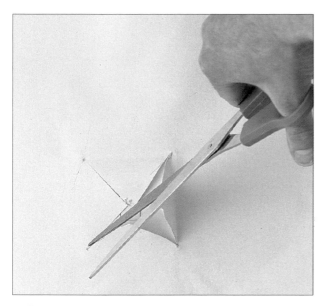

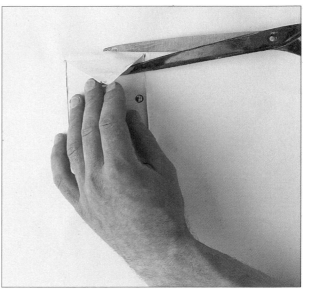

4 Using scissors, carefully make four diagonal cuts from the center of the switch out to the pencil marks.

5 Trim off each of the four flaps just inside the outer edges of the switch so a small overlap remains over the switch plate.

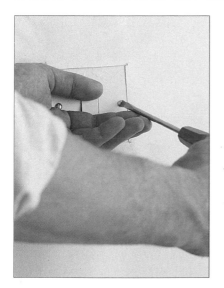

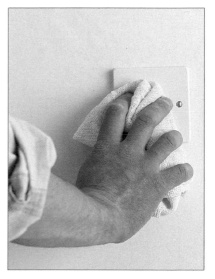

6 Loosen the two screws that hold the switch plate in place. It's not necessary to unscrew them completely—just loosen the screws enough so that you can move the plate away from the wall.

7 Ease the switch plate away from the wall, rotating it slightly from side to side. Be careful not to tear the paper when pushing the plate through it. Use the brush to push the paper behind the plate.

8 Wipe up any excess paste with a dry cloth. Put the switch plate back and tighten the screws, making sure the small paper flaps are firmly tucked behind the plate. Be careful not to overtighten the screws.

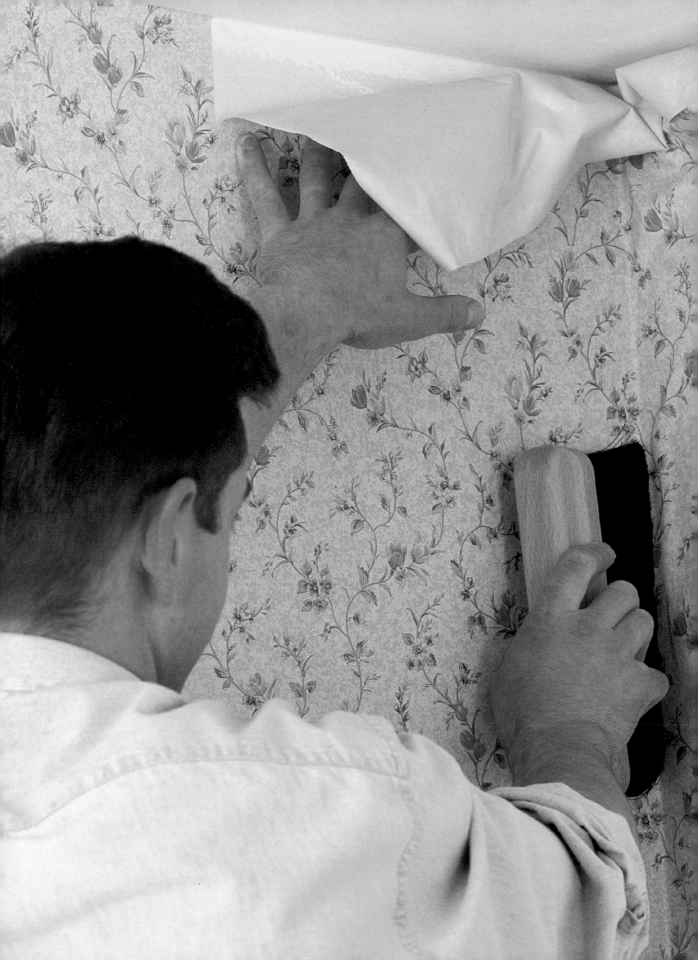

Wallpapering

Hanging the wallpaper itself can be the most enjoyable part of the job. Although there's a huge variety of papers, most are hung the same way. This chapter explains the whole process, from where to start to papering around obstructions. Always read the wallpaper manufacturer's instructions for any specific requirements for your paper.

Where to start

Where you start papering depends on the shape and layout of the room and on your wallpaper design. Is there a focal point, such as a fireplace? If so, and you're using a large pattern, the pattern will need to be centered. With smaller or free-match patterns, this isn't necessary. In these situations, it's best to start close to a corner on a wall that doesn't have any windows or doors.

TOOLS: Stepladder, tape measure, pencil, level, hammer, nail, plumb line

MATERIALS: Wallpaper

CHECKING THE PAPER

Colors from different dye lots can vary, so make sure the lot number on each roll is the same. Unwrap one of the rolls and check for any pattern imperfections or shading differences in the paper. If you find any problems, they're likely to be present in the rest of the rolls, too. Manufacturers may not accept liability if more than one roll is opened, so don't skip this spot check.

CENTERING

Correct centering of your wallpaper will create a well-balanced effect. Achieving this takes planning because some wall coverings have the central pattern joining on a seam, while others put it in the middle of the length or even slightly off center within the length.

The best way to center the pattern is to hold an unpasted cut length in what will be its approximate centered position above the fireplace mantelpiece.

Make a pencil mark at the side of this length of paper, and then draw a vertical guideline with a level. When you're ready to hang this first length, you will use this pencil line to correctly position the paper. Next, use a tape measure and a level to make any final adjustments, making sure the main pattern is centered over the fireplace. After hanging the first length, complete the fireplace wall before starting on the rest of the room.

▲ Poor centering can result in an unbalanced look.

▲ The balanced look of correct centering.

WHERE TO START

CENTERING NECESSARY

1 First length
2 Finish fireplace
3 Complete room

NO CENTERING NECESSARY

1 First length
2 Continue around room
3 Final length to join in corner

USING A PLUMB LINE

A plumb line gives you a reliable vertical guideline. Hammer a small nail into the wall close to the ceiling, and hang the plumb line. Make a series of pencil marks along the length of the string, and use a steel rule to connect them.

NO CENTERING NECESSARY

1 If pattern centering isn't necessary, start near an inside corner. Measure 1 inch less than your wallpaper's width away from the corner, and make a mark with a pencil.

2 Place a long level vertically against this mark and draw a pencil line down its length. This is where you'll position the first length of paper, which you'll hang on the opposite side of the line to the corner—not toward the corner. On the other side of the pencil line, you'll have allowed for a 1-inch overlap. You'll use it when you've papered all the way around the room and need to make a seam in the corner (see the diagram above).

Measuring and cutting

Careful measuring will prevent expensive mistakes (if you cut the paper too short) and unnecessary waste (if you cut it too long). Your job will be easier if you're using a free-match paper, such as vertical stripes, where no pattern matching is necessary. But you'll need to be more careful when hanging patterned papers, especially those with a large repeat.

TOOLS: Pasting table, tape measure, pencil, steel rule, scissors

MATERIALS: Wallpaper

MEASURING SMALL REPEATS

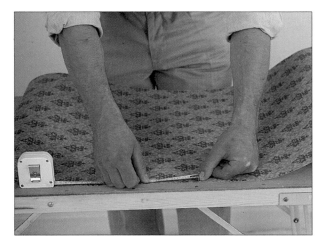

With small repeat patterns—about 2 to 4 inches— it's best to add 4 inches to the wall height (that is, two times 2 inches). This addition allows for trimming at each end, plus the length of the repeat. By working in this way, you can cut a number of standard lengths at once; otherwise, you'll find yourself stopping to measure, cut, and paste every length of paper.

    If you do cut several lengths at once, be sure to check first that the ceiling height is consistent all the way around the room.

MEASURING LARGE REPEATS

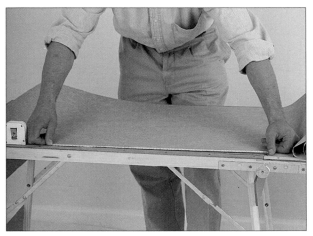

One option for larger patterns is to match the next length (unpasted) to the previous one, and cut it to the right size with enough left over for trimming. This may take longer but will create less waste, especially for offset patterns. Always use this technique to cut lengths for small areas.

MEASURING PATTERN REPEAT

Most manufacturers print the size of the pattern repeat on the roll label. Even so, it's always best to check the size yourself and get an exact measurement.

1 Measure the exact height of the wall from the ceiling to the top of the baseboard.

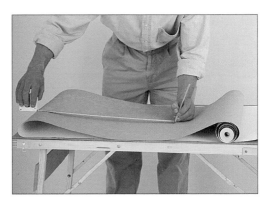

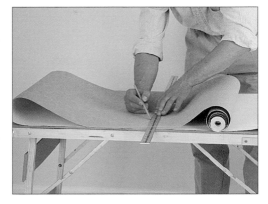

2 Unroll the paper on the pasting table. It's usually necessary to fold the paper back on itself for measuring, since most lengths will be longer than the table. Make a small mark with a pencil at the length you need.

3 Always try to keep the edge of the paper flush with the long edge of your worktable so your cuts will be square. Line a straightedge on the pencil mark and draw a line across the width of the paper.

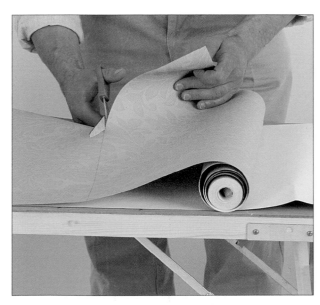

4 Use scissors to make a straight cut along the pencil line. It doesn't need to be perfectly even, since you'll trim this end.

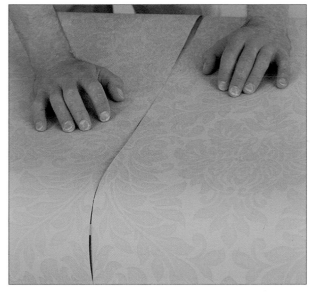

5 Before hanging the first length, practice matching the pattern; some are subtle and difficult to see.

Pasting

Most wallpaper is hung one of three ways. Prepasted paper is soaked in water to activate the paste. Other papers are hung unpasted because the paste is applied to the wall. But the most common type uses special wallpaper paste that's brushed on the paper before hanging. The pasting itself is easy as long as you keep the length of paper clean and avoid tearing it or getting paste where you don't want it.

TOOLS: Pasting table, 2 buckets, stirring stick, sponge, liquid measuring cup, pasting brush, paper-hanging brush, scissors

MATERIALS: Wallpaper, paste, water

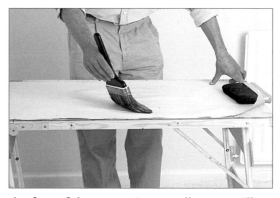

1 Before mixing the paste, make sure all your equipment is clean. Measure the right amount of cold water into the bucket, following the paste manufacturer's directions. Slowly sprinkle the paste into the water, stirring vigorously to mix it well. Most pastes should be stirred for 2 to 3 minutes after all powder has been added. Let the paste stand for 2 to 3 minutes more, give it another quick stir, and it's ready to use.

2 Unroll the paper and weight it down to keep it from rolling back up; a paper-hanging brush works well for this. Be sure to line up the edge of the paper with the table edge so you don't get paste on the face of the paper. Some wallpapers will stain if paste dries on them, so wipe up spills with a damp sponge. Apply the paste evenly, brushing from the center out and covering the entire surface with a thin film of paste.

USING THE RIGHT PASTE

Always use the specific paste recommended for your wallpaper. The chemical composition of some pastes makes them suitable only for particular papers. Paste is available in two forms: premixed and powdered. Although premixed paste is convenient, it's more economical—and quite easy—to mix your own.

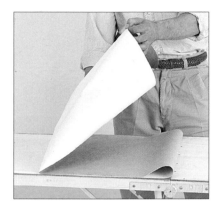

3 Most lengths will tend to be longer than the table. Once the area of paper covering the table has been pasted, gently fold the pasted end over on itself, accordion-style.

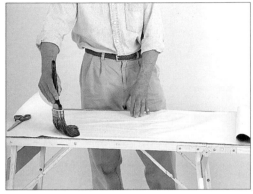

4 Move the bundle of folded, pasted paper back along the table so that the bundle lies at one end and frees up your work area. Again, use a weight to anchor the unpasted end of the paper while you paste the rest of the length.

SOAKING TIME
All pasted wallpaper needs to soak for up to 15 minutes; always check the manufacturer's directions for the exact length of time. Soaking allows the paper to expand and become more pliable so it will be less likely to bubble as it dries.

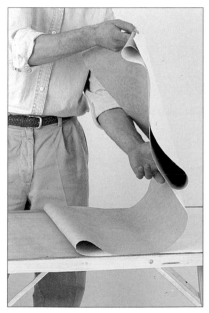

5 With the entire length now pasted, continue to fold it into a bundle. Try to support the paper as you fold it and avoid creasing it. Creases will be visible when the paper is hung.

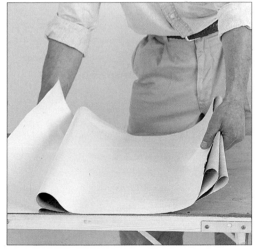

6 Carefully pick up the folded bundle and set it aside for the required soaking time. On the back of the paper, write the time it will be ready to be applied to the wall. This will ensure that all lengths get the same soaking time and will help keep them in the right order if you have several lengths soaking at the same time.

7 After pasting each length, wipe the pasting table down with a clean, damp sponge. This avoids getting leftover paste on the patterned side of the next length you lay on the table.

Prepasted and paste-the-wall papers

Prepasted paper is becoming more popular, mainly because it's so easy to use. When the paper is made, dry paste is added to the back. The paste is reactivated with water by soaking the paper in a trough before it's hung.

Many manufacturers recommend putting the trough on the floor so you can pull the paper out and hang it directly on the wall. But this may cause problems with some papers. The technique shown here will work with all types of prepasted papers.

Other wall coverings are designed to be hung by applying paste to the wall instead of to the paper. They're called paste-the-wall papers.

TOOLS: Pasting table, wallpaper trough, bucket, sponge, pasting brush or roller, paper-hanging brush

MATERIALS: Wallpaper, paste, water

PASTE-THE-WALL PAPER

1 Using a pasting brush or a paint roller, thoroughly apply paste to an area slightly wider than the paper.

2 When the paste is spread evenly, hang the paper directly from the roll or cut it to length first (see pages 54–55).

PREPASTED PAPER

2 Fill the trough two-thirds full with cold water and set it at one end of your work surface. With both hands, put the roll of paper in the trough, holding the paper under the water for the manufacturer's recommended soaking time. Wiggle the roll slightly during soaking to eliminate any air bubbles and to make sure all of the paper is getting evenly wet.

1 Measure and cut the paper in the usual way (see pages 54–55). On the pasting table, loosely roll up the cut length of paper against its natural curl from the roll so the prepasted side faces out.

3 Carefully pull the soaked paper out of the water and onto the worktable with its patterned side facing down. Let any excess water drain back into the trough. If the paper needs further soaking, go to steps 4 and 5, described below. Otherwise, fold up the bottom end of the paper, placing its pasted sides together. This will make it much easier for you when carrying the paper and applying it to the wall.

4 If more soaking is needed, fold the top half of the paper back on itself as far as the middle of the length, pasted sides together, keeping the paper edges flush.

5 Fold the bottom half to the center. This promotes even paste coverage and keeps the paper moist until it's ready to hang. Use a damp sponge to clean the table between soaking the lengths.

EXTRA PASTE
Although prepasted paper doesn't need traditional wallpaper paste, it's often helpful to keep a small amount on hand for edges that dry out. When hanging a length that requires time-consuming cutting (such as around an ornate mantelpiece or an archway), you can add more paste wherever it's needed to make sure all edges are firmly adhered.

Hanging the first length

Before hanging the first length of paper, check which way it should go. With some patterns, the direction may seem not to matter, but when the paper is on the wall, mistakes can be glaring. Manufacturers of free-match patterns often recommend reversing every other length to even out any minor differences in shading. Always read the instructions for your particular paper.

Take your time when hanging the first length, not only to make sure it's level, but also to get the pattern correctly positioned and centered, especially with large designs (see pages 52–53).

TOOLS: Pasting table, 2 buckets, sponge, pasting brush, paper-hanging brush, wallpaper trough (if needed), stepladder, scissors

MATERIALS: Wallpaper, paste, water

1 Position the first length of paper on the wall next to your pencil guideline (see pages 52–53). The top of the length should be at the wall-ceiling line with a 2-inch overlap onto the ceiling for trimming. Be careful not to tear the paper when you unfold it.

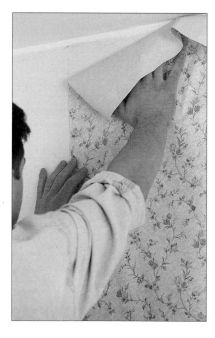

2 Now that the top section of the length is loosely attached to the wall at the correct height, slide the vertical edge of the paper into its final position next to the vertical pencil guideline.

3 Using the paper-hanging brush, firmly push the top edge of the paper into the wall-ceiling junction. As you push the paper, make sure the paper doesn't move out of its correct vertical alignment.

4 Move down the length of paper, brushing out any air bubbles or creases and working from the center to the edges. Keep checking that the vertical edge of the paper is still aligned with the guideline.

5 When the top half of the paper is hung in its final position, leave the bottom section untouched for now. Instead, return to the wall-ceiling junction and begin trimming the top portion of the paper.

6 Run the blunt edge of your scissors along the paper crease at the wall-ceiling junction to create a guideline to trim by. You also can use a pencil to make your line.

7 Pull the paper away from the wall and trim it with scissors along the creased guideline. If you find the ceiling slightly uneven, trim just above the crease for a better fit.

8 With the paper-hanging brush, push the trimmed edge back into the wall-ceiling junction. Add a little extra paste if the edge has started to dry out during trimming.

Finishing the first length

When the top half of the first length of wallpaper is in position and trimmed at the top (see pages 60–61), you can start work on the bottom section that hasn't yet been pasted to the wall.

At the bottom of a wall, uneven wall-baseboard junctions often are a problem. To get around them, call on the same technique you used for trimming at an uneven ceiling: Cut slightly below the creased trim line to allow for undulations in the wall and make a neater edge.

TOOLS: Pasting table, 2 buckets, sponge, pasting brush, paper-hanging brush, wallpaper trough (if needed), scissors, stepladder, crafts knife, rotary trimmer

MATERIALS: Wallpaper, paste, water

1 When the top half of the paper is securely in place and the top edge is trimmed to fit, ease the bottom half of the paper away from the wall, releasing its folds as necessary.

2 Using the paper-hanging brush, work downward, freeing air bubbles and smoothing out the paper. Firmly push the paper into the wall-baseboard junction.

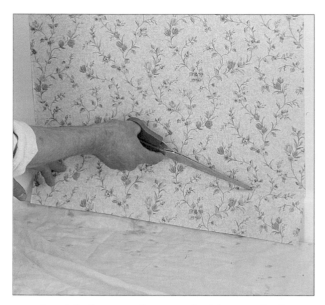

3 As with the top edge, use the blunt end of your scissors or a pencil to crease a trim line along the junction between the wall and the baseboard. (See Step 6 on page 61.)

4 Pull the paper back and trim along the creased guideline. Then use the paper-hanging brush to push the paper's edge back into the wall-baseboard junction.

5 Finally, use a clean, damp sponge to wipe excess paste from the ceiling, baseboard, and the wallpaper itself.

IDEAL TOOLS

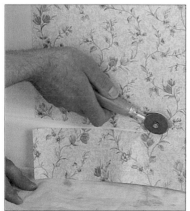

Crafts knife
May be used for trimming instead of scissors. For safety, cut in a direction away from your body. Change the blade regularly for the cleanest cuts.

Rotary trimmer
Also handy for cutting paper by running the circular blade along the guide crease. Use a dry cloth to keep the blade clean and free of paste buildup.

Pattern matching

When butt joints are done properly, most wallpaper patterns match fairly well from one length to the next, making it practically impossible to see the seam.

There are three types of patterns you may need to match: Free-match patterns have no specific place where the lengths join; straight-match patterns do have a specific place where lengths join; and offset-match patterns stagger the pattern between lengths and also have a precise joining location. To match an intricate pattern, just follow the steps shown here.

TOOLS: Pasting table, 2 buckets, sponge, pasting brush, paper-hanging brush, wallpaper trough (if needed), stepladder, scissors, crafts knife, seam roller, level

MATERIALS: Wallpaper, paste, water

1 Paste the new length of paper and carefully position it on the wall as close to the pattern match as possible.

2 With the pasted paper hanging loosely on the wall, slide the top half of the length flush against the previous length, forming a tight butt joint. At the same time, work with your hands to make any minor vertical adjustments to create a perfect pattern match.

3 Brush the paper as usual, paying special attention to the edges of the seam in order to create a smooth finish and tight fit. Make sure that the paper remains closely butted together and that the wallpaper pattern matches consistently all the way down to the baseboard.

AVOIDING DRY EDGES

Wallpaper edges can dry out due to insufficient pasting or when trimming an awkward, time-consuming area. Keep your pasting brush handy to add more paste where necessary.

DEALING WITH PATTERN DROP

Problems with matching patterns are especially common with hand-printed papers. Because of the way these papers are manufactured, some may show variations in pattern size or consistency throughout the roll. By the time the paper reaches the lower part of a wall, the pattern may have "dropped." If this happens, simply match the pattern at eye level rather than at the top so the area you'll see most often has the best pattern match.

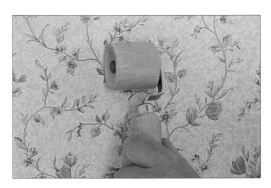

4 Gently run a seam roller down the butt joint to ensure good adhesion and a perfectly flat seam. Don't use a seam roller over embossed papers, because they can flatten the raised designs.

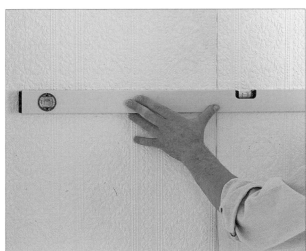

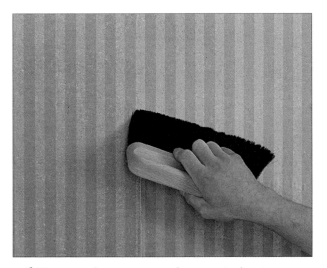

5 Some papers are hard to get perfectly level. On some straight-match papers, the actual joint may be a free match. For example, the paper may have a floral pattern in the center, but the edges may join on a vertical stripe design. If necessary, use a level to check horizontal alignment.

6 Free-match patterns, such as vertical stripes, are the easiest to join because no particular match is necessary. However, work carefully to make sure the butt joint is tight, because free-match patterns will reveal seam problems that busier floral designs might disguise.

Inside corners

All rooms have inside corners, so learning the best way to paper them just makes sense. A common mistake—trying to fold wallpaper around an inside corner—often results in poor adhesion along the entire corner crease. Worse, the wallpaper may come out of alignment because the corner isn't perfectly square. Instead, it's best to cut the paper into two vertical strips and hang each separately to get the paper to turn smoothly from one wall to the next.

TOOLS: Pasting table, 2 buckets, sponge, pasting brush, paper-hanging brush, wallpaper trough (if needed), stepladder, tape measure, scissors, crafts knife, level, brush

MATERIALS: Wallpaper, paste, water, overlap adhesive

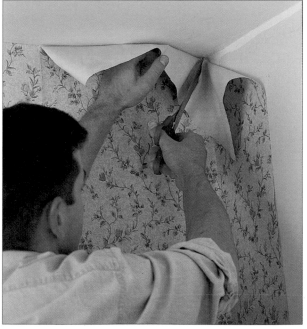

1 At an inside corner, match the pattern and brush out the paper as usual, but only to the corner crease. Let the paper that folds around the corner loosely stick to the wall. This will make it easier to push the paper into the corner.

2 Use scissors to make a diagonal cut into the junction where the wall, ceiling, and corner meet. The cut should extend as far as the corner. Make a similar cut at floor level into the junction at the baseboard and the corner.

3 Use a crafts knife to make a vertical cut from the ceiling to the floor, allowing a ¼- to ½-inch overlap onto the unpapered wall. It's often easiest to start and finish this cut with a pair of scissors.

4 Remove the cut section and hang it temporarily on the unpapered wall. Return to the other part and trim the top and bottom, making sure the paper is pasted tightly in the corner.

5 Move the cut section so that it overlaps the hung section down the entire length of the corner, matching the pattern as closely as possible as you work. With vinyl coverings, it may be necessary to use a stronger adhesive to bond the corner overlap. If so, pull back the paper along the corner and apply overlap adhesive, either straight from the tube or using a brush. Then firmly push the paper back into position.

6 To hang the second strip, use a level to make sure you're starting the next wall with a perfectly vertical edge. When the position is correct, trim the top and bottom as usual. Finally, sponge the corner thoroughly, because overlaps always leave paste on the surface.

CHECKING THE HORIZONTAL

With some straight-match papers, you also may need to use a level across the corner to check for horizontal alignment.

Outside corners

It's rare to find a perfectly square outside corner. So when you paper around them, you may need to realign the paper so it's once again vertical. You can do this simply by overlapping the new length onto the previous one, but the overlap probably will show.

As shown earlier with lining paper, making an overlapping butt joint is a better alternative (see pages 42–43). Having to match a pattern makes the job a bit more tricky than hanging lining paper, but if you follow these steps, you can be sure of professional results.

TOOLS: Pasting table, 2 buckets, sponge, pasting brush, paper-hanging brush, wallpaper trough (if needed), stepladder, tape measure, scissors, crafts knife, steel rule, seam roller, level

MATERIALS: Wallpaper, paste, water

1 When approaching an outside corner, hang the paper as usual and bend the excess around the corner using the paper-hanging brush to work out any bubbles and to ensure good adhesion along the corner edge. Allow the section around the corner to attach loosely to the center of the wall. Don't apply too much pressure to the paper above or below this point or you could tear it at ceiling or floor level.

2 Using scissors, make a diagonal cut into the baseboard-corner junction and then at the ceiling-corner junction. Now it will be easier to smooth the paper on each side of the corner.

3 Trim the top and bottom of the wall covering, checking to be sure that there are no bubbles along the corner. If the new starting edge is perfectly vertical, you're ready to hang the next length. Usually, however, the paper edge won't be vertical. In that case, follow Steps 4 through 8 on the opposite page.

4 Use a craft knife to trim the paper back to the corner leaving a 1½-inch overlap around the corner.

5 Hang another length of paper, covering the trimmed overlap with the edge of the new piece. Be aware, however, that you'll probably need to make some adjustments, because this rough wallpaper joint will be easy to see and could be an eyesore. For a neater appearance, move the new length of wallpaper so that it still overlaps the previous length but also matches the pattern exactly. The width of the wallpaper's design will determine the degree to which you need to overlap the two lengths of paper. When the new piece of wallpaper is in place, make sure the new length is level, even if you have to make a small compromise in the pattern match a bit. Trim the new length at top and bottom, as usual.

6 Place a steel rule vertically on the corner ¾ inch from the edge, then use a crafts knife to cut carefully through the two lengths of overlapping wallpaper. Slide the straightedge along and continue cutting down the wallpaper to the baseboard.

7 Carefully pull back this cut edge on the overlapping piece of wallpaper, and gently remove the two strips of excess paper that are stuck on top of each other. Be careful not to damage the top edge; you'll need it to make a tight joint.

8 Push the edge back together using a paper-hanging brush. You'll have a perfect butt joint with the pattern still matching. A seam roller can help you make a totally flat joint. Finally, use a clean, damp sponge to remove excess paste.

Doors and obstructions

Papering around anything that stands out from the wall, such as a door, window, or a fireplace, calls for skillful trimming to get professional results. Fortunately, as with most wallpapering tasks, this requires more time and patience than artistry, per se.

Part of the trick is knowing what direction to make the cuts. For this, a sharp crafts knife is essential; keep the blade free of wallpaper paste and change it often.

TOOLS: Pasting table, 2 buckets, sponge, pasting brush, paper-hanging brush, wallpaper trough (if needed), stepladder, scissors, crafts knife

MATERIALS: Wallpaper, paste, water, clean cloth

FIREPLACES

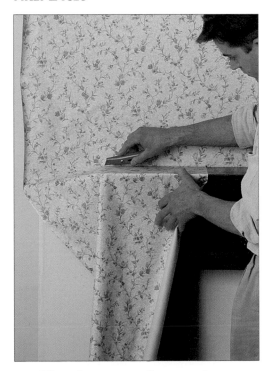

1 Allow the paper to flop over the top of the fireplace and push it into the wall-mantelpiece junction using the paper-hanging brush. Use a crafts knife to cut from the top corner of the fireplace along the creased edge.

2 Put a finger on the corner of the cut and pick up the paper flap, gently molding it into the angles with the paper-hanging brush. Make a series of right-angle cuts into the finely detailed areas.

3 Carefully trim each of the small flaps, using a crafts knife and being careful not to damage or scratch the moldings underneath the paper.

4 Smooth the paper into its final position. With a clean sponge or cloth, remove any excess paste from the fireplace to avoid staining the surface.

DOORS

1 When you get to a door, it's best to start by matching the pattern near the ceiling and then allow the rest of the wallpaper to fall loosely over the door trim. Using the paper-hanging brush, push the paper firmly into the top of the trim.

2 Use your finger to mark the point where the corner of the trim meets the wall, and using the scissors, make a diagonal cut to this point. As you near the final point, move your finger back slightly to support the paper.

3 As you work down the length of the door, continue to match the wallpaper pattern with the previous length of paper. Then, push the vertical overlapping edge firmly into the junction of the wall and the door trim. Make sure you don't let the paper move, or you could inadvertently break the pattern match with the previous length.

4 Trim the two flaps with a crafts knife. Hold the blade at a 45-degree angle to the wall surface, keeping it as steady as possible. By making the cut slightly onto the trim, you'll find it easier to keep a straight line; many junctions between the wall and the trim are uneven. Remember to wipe excess paste off the woodwork immediately.

Recessed windows

The job of papering a recessed window combines many of the techniques already shown in this chapter. However, you'll still need to carefully plan the order of papering steps that you take. Because wall coverings on recessed windows often are exposed to moisture, as well as to a wide range of temperatures, you'll also want to make sure that all edges of the paper are pasted down firmly.

Although it takes some effort to get perfect seams around recessed windows, minor mistakes are easy to conceal with curtains or blinds.

TOOLS: Pasting table, 2 buckets, sponge, pasting brush, paper-hanging brush, wallpaper trough (if needed), stepladder, tape measure, scissors, crafts knife, steel rule, seam roller

MATERIALS: Wallpaper, paste, water

1 When you get to the window, carefully match the pattern on the length of new paper with what you've already hung. Then, allow the paper to drop over the window recess. Make sure the wallpaper on the top and side of the recess is firmly pasted down.

2 Make two horizontal cuts in the paper back to the corners. At the bottom, use the windowsill as a guide. Then at the top, use the recess edge. Don't let the paper tear under its own weight. Attach the flap loosely to the wall of the recess.

3 Use a pair of scissors to make a series of right-angle cuts into the profile of the bottom corner of the windowsill. This will let the paper mold around and under the sill so you can position and trim the bottom half of the length.

4 Now use the technique for papering outside corners on pages 68–69 to bend the flap of paper around and into the recess. Push the paper firmly into the junction between the wall and the window frame, and trim all areas as usual.

5 Cut the next length to extend from the ceiling around the top of the recess to the top of the frame. Hang it to overlap the previous length, matching the pattern. Mark the recess corner with your finger; make a diagonal cut to this point.

6 Now make an overlapping butt joint. Use a steel rule and a crafts knife to cut a diagonal line through the area where the two pieces overlap. Make sure the line goes through the busiest part of the pattern to conceal the seam.

7 Peel back the paper and discard the top section of the first length. Remove the bottom section of the new length, and push the pieces back together to produce a perfect butt joint.

8 Bend the remaining flap of paper around the top recess, holding the paper at the recess corner to avoid tearing. Notice that in Step 5, you made a diagonal cut. This will let you tuck a small overlap of this section behind the flap on the side recess wall, making a neater seam. Finally, trim and clean all areas with a damp sponge. Complete the rest of the window the same way.

Stairwells

Your main concern when papering a stairwell is safety. For a stable working platform, you can rent scaffolding designed specifically for stairwells. Or, with a little ingenuity, you can build your own platform. Just make sure the boards you use are strong enough to support your weight, and tie them to the ladders with rope.

Because you'll be working with long lengths of paper, this job is done much easier with two people.

TOOLS: Ladders, boards, rope, paper-hanging equipment, level, tape measure, scissors, crafts knife

MATERIALS: Wallpaper, paste, water, masking tape, soft cloths

Making a platform

Attach your boards to the stepladder and ladder(s) with rope to keep them from slipping. Make sure the boards are strong; scaffolding boards are best for this purpose. If you're bridging a gap of 5 feet or more, tie two boards together, one on top of the other, for extra strength.

For spans that are longer than 8 to 10 feet, provide extra support in the middle of the platform. Adjustable ladders, which let you make one side longer than the other, are excellent for setting up on steps.

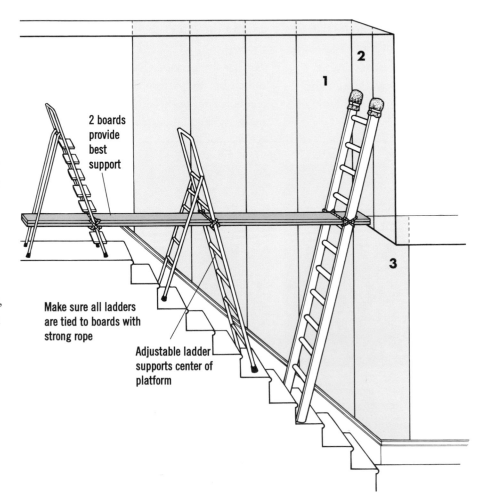

2 boards provide best support

Make sure all ladders are tied to boards with strong rope

Adjustable ladder supports center of platform

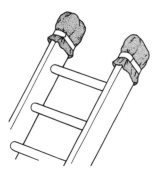

Protecting the wall

To avoid damaging new paper, pad the ends of the ladder. Use soft cloths held in place with masking tape or commercially available ladder pads.

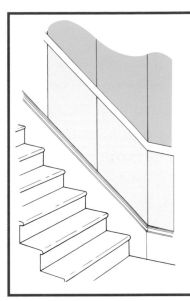

Divided walls

The lower levels of paper usually get the most wear and tear. By using two papers or even painting the lower wall section, you can avoid redecorating the entire stairwell, replacing just the bottom section.

Order of work

Start hanging the paper with the longest length. It's important to make your first length perfectly vertical because a small error at the top will be greatly magnified by the time you reach the bottom of the length. Use a plumb line to find a true vertical.

By working up the stairs as shown at right, measuring subsequent lengths is easier than if you worked down the stairs.

When you've hung all the lengths to the left of point 1 in the drawing opposite and on the other side of the wall (if you're papering it, too), you can take down the platform and use just the extension ladder to hang the lengths from point 2.

As shown above, padding the ends of the ladder will avoid damaging the new paper you've just hung.

Finally, remove the ladder and continue from point 3 to finish the other walls downstairs. Then finish any papering on the upper floor.

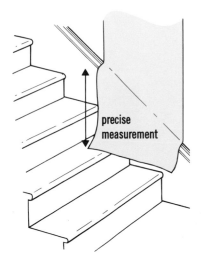

precise measurement

Papering up stairs

The shape of the walls above staircases can waste a lot of paper. It's easy to make measuring mistakes if you work down the stairs because you can only estimate where the end of the paper will fall. To avoid expensive mistakes, it's easier to work from the longest length back up the stairs, as described and shown at left.

PATTERNS

Certain patterns work better than others in stairwells. For example, stripes can make an already high wall seem even taller. A busy pattern, on the other hand, not only matches well but also minimizes the risk of pattern-drop problems or the unavoidable overlaps on such a wide, open expanse of wall area.

Archways

Wallpapering around a curved arch isn't as difficult as it may seem. Of course, matching the wallpaper pattern is more complicated, so it's always best to avoid papers that are tricky to match. Also avoid vertical stripes; the curve of an arch will wreak havoc with their direction.

Busy mini prints or floral wallpaper patterns are ideal for rooms or hallways that contain arches, because they draw the eye to the shape of the architecture and not to any mistakes or overlaps at seams and corners.

TOOLS: Pasting table, 2 buckets, sponge, pasting brush, paper-hanging brush, wallpaper trough (if needed), stepladder, crafts knife, scissors, tape measure, brush

MATERIALS: Wallpaper, paste, water, seam adhesive

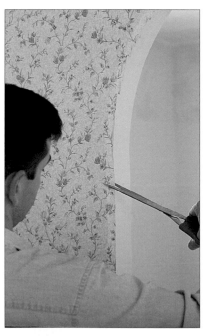

1 Let the first length hang over the arch. Pattern-match it to the previous length as usual, and make sure the paper is firmly pasted down around the top and sides of the arch.

2 Use a pair of scissors to trim the paper that is hanging in the arch, cutting back to 1 inch from the edges of the arch. Support the paper to make a more accurate cut.

3 Working just around the curved part of the archway, use scissors to make a series of cuts perpendicular to the edge of the arch. Space them about ½ inch apart.

5 Before papering the inside of the archway itself, paper the wall on the other side of the arch. For the curved surface, cut a strip of paper 1¼ inches wider than the width of the arch. With a free-match pattern, you may be able to use one length of paper for the whole arch. However, if the paper has a definite "right side up," you'll need to join two lengths at the highest point to avoid having the pattern run upside down on one side. Line up the factory edge of the paper strip with the edge of the archway to keep the pattern in vertical alignment. Initially, trim only at the baseboard.

4 Brush and smooth the small flaps of paper around the curve and the rest of the overlap on the vertical edge of the arch. Hang the next lengths of paper on the wall above the arch, using the same technique to paper the curve.

6 With a sharp crafts knife, trim the paper along the arch edge by holding the flat blade of the knife up against the edge of the arch and steadily cutting down. Hang the second length on the other side of the arch in the same way. Where the two lengths meet at the top of the arch, make an overlapping butt joint using a steel rule as shown on pages 72–73.

7 Because of the unavoidable overlaps you'll make when papering an arch, you may need seam adhesive to paste down problem areas. Use a brush to apply it, and remember to sponge off the excess.

Wall-mounted fixtures

Because it can be difficult to hang wallpaper around wall-mounted fixtures, such as lights and radiators, it's best to remove them if at all possible. In old homes with radiators, old pipes and frozen joints may force you to make the best of the situation.

Most light fixtures are easy to take down. For those that aren't, be careful to keep paste off brass and other fixture hardware that might easily stain.

For information on papering around wall switches and outlets, see pages 48–49.

TOOLS: Pasting table, 2 buckets, sponge, pasting brush, paper-hanging brush, wallpaper trough (if needed), stepladder, tape measure, crafts knife, scissors, pencil, roller, screwdriver

MATERIALS: Wallpaper, paste, water, electrical tape

RADIATORS

1 Let the wallpaper fall over the top of the radiator, making sure the top of the length of paper is correctly matched and joined to the previous piece. Pull the paper back slightly and, using a pencil, mark the location of the support bracket.

2 Using a pair of scissors, make a vertical cut from the bottom of the wallpaper just to the pencil mark. Inevitably, you will get some wallpaper paste on the radiator, but you can wipe it off when you're finished papering the wall behind it.

3 Using a roller, push the paper in place on each side of the support bracket. Trim the paper below the radiator, and wipe any excess paste from all surfaces. Repeat steps 1–3 to paper around the other bracket.

LIGHT FIXTURES

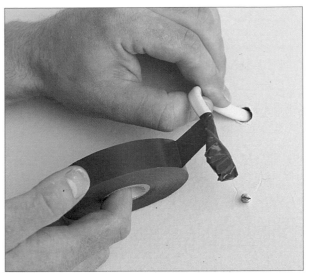

1 For safety, turn off the power at your electrical box before removing any light fixtures. Then, unscrew the wall-mounted fixture, supporting its weight until it's free of the wall.

2 Using electrical tape, cover the exposed wires. Replace the screws in the wall. You may want to draw a diagram of the wiring connections to help you replace the fixture.

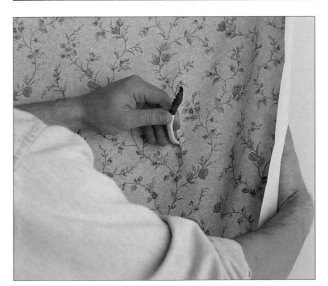

3 Let the wallpaper fall over the fixture area. Use a pencil to mark the spot where the wire leaves the wall. With scissors, make a small cut in the paper on this mark, then carefully thread the wire through the hole.

4 Using a paper-hanging brush, smooth out the paper, letting the wall screws break through the paper surface. Trim the rest of the paper where necessary. Let the paper dry out before you replace the fixture.

Ceilings

The technique for papering a ceiling is much like the one used for lining a ceiling (see pages 36–37), except that patterns make matching alignment a bit trickier. Although it's much easier to paper a ceiling with two people, you can do the job on your own if you take your time—especially when hanging the first length.

When using an embossed paper on your ceilings or walls, as shown on these two pages, be careful to not apply too much pressure to the surface of the paper or you may flatten the embossed design.

TOOLS: Sawhorses and boards, pasting table, 2 buckets, sponge, pasting brush, paper-hanging brush, wallpaper trough (if needed), scissors, tape measure, chalk line, hammer, crafts knife

MATERIALS: Wallpaper, paste, water, 2 nails, chalk

1 Decide on the direction in which you'll hang the lengths, and set up a work platform. Measure out from the side wall the exact width of the paper, minus a 1-inch overlap onto the wall. Do this at both ends of the first length. This will allow both for any unevenness at the ceiling-wall junction and for trimming.

2 A chalk line snapped against the ceiling makes a nice, long guideline for hanging the first length of wall covering. At each end of the width that you've measured in the previous step, hammer a small nail into the ceiling. Don't sink the nails too far or they'll be hard to remove.

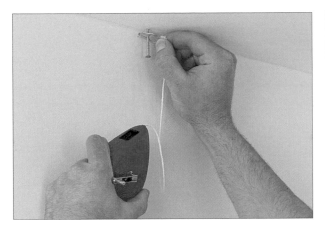

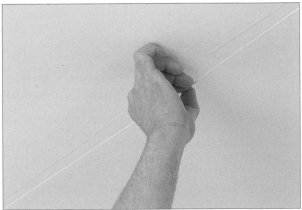

3 It's best to work with a commercially available chalk line. However, if you don't want to purchase one, household string dusted with colored chalk also will work. Attach the line to the nails, making sure it's taut.

4 From the center of the platform, pull the line down about 2 to 4 inches from the ceiling and then release it. The snapping action will leave a straight chalk line on the ceiling. Remove the line and the nails.

5 Begin hanging your wallpaper at the junction between the wall and the ceiling, using the chalk guideline to carefully position the edge of the first length of paper. This should leave the planned 1-inch overlap of wallpaper on the adjacent wall as measured in Step 1.

6 Use the paper-hanging brush to brush out bubbles beneath the surface and to push the paper into the wall-ceiling junction. If necessary, refer back to pages 36–37 for more about trimming. When this first length is up, the others go much more quickly.

Borders

You can dramatically change the appearance of a room with a border, whether you apply it over wallpaper or to a painted surface. Regardless of how high you hang your border, it's important to get it perfectly level or it can disrupt the rest of your room. Border adhesive usually dries quickly, so always work on just one wall at a time, and never attempt to go all the way around a room with one continuous strip of paper.

TOOLS: Pasting table, bucket, sponge, small pasting brush, paper-hanging brush, level, scissors, tape measure, pencil

MATERIALS: Border, border adhesive, water

1 Measure from the top of the baseboard to the height at which you want the top or bottom of the border, and then make a mark with a pencil. From this mark, use a level to draw a guideline around the room. Don't press too hard with the pencil or the line may show through the border after you've pasted it in place.

2 Measure the width of the first wall, adding a 2-inch overlap at each end. Cut this length and, using a small brush, apply the border adhesive to the reverse side. Fold the border into a bundle (see pages 56–57) and let it soak for the required time.

3 Starting in one corner of the first wall, hang the border on the wall. Let the 2-inch overlap go around the corner and onto the adjacent wall. The border edge should follow the pencil line, slightly overlapping it so the marks won't be visible when the border is hung.

SELF-ADHESIVE BORDERS
These are easy to use; just peel away the backing paper. Although they make less mess when installing and are easy to remove, it can be tricky to adjust them once they're stuck down.

4 Continue to the other corner, brushing out any air bubbles and making sure the border is perfectly level. Again, let the 2-inch overlap go around the corner.

5 In both corners, use a pair of scissors to trim the paper back and leave a ¼-inch overlap on the adjacent wall. Then sponge the border to remove any excess adhesive.

6 Pattern-match the end of the next length of dry border to the corner that you have just completed. Next, roll out the dry border along the length of the wall to determine the length you need. Again, add a single 2-inch overlap (not 4 inches as in Step 2). Paste the new length of border, and hang it as before. Match the pattern in the corner by letting the new length overlap the old one. When you have positioned the border correctly, score the corner crease with a pair of scissors, peel back the new length, and cut directly along the creased guideline.

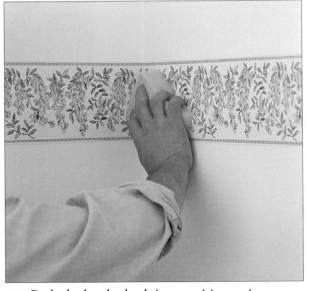

7 Push the border back into position, using a sponge to remove any excess adhesive. The small overlap that you left on the previous length reduces the chance of a line or a gap appearing in the corner, especially if the corner isn't square. The overlap improves the finish and is practically invisible once you've finished. Hang the rest of the border the same way.

Divisions and miters

Borders can provide a decorative division between different wallpapers or highlight the features of a room, such as the frame of a window. For a neat appearance, you'll want to miter the horizontal and vertical lengths where they meet. Because you won't be able to pattern-match the border exactly on each joint, choose your border carefully; busy florals tend to hide matching inconsistencies better than symmetrical designs.

TOOLS: Pasting table, bucket, sponge, small pasting brush, paper-hanging brush, stepladder, scissors, tape measure, pencil, crafts knife, steel rule, level

MATERIALS: Border, border adhesive, water

BORDER DIVISIONS

2 Using the level of the pencil line on the wall as a guide, cut through the overlapping papers. Remove the excess strips, creating an overlapping butt joint. (This is similar to the technique on pages 68–69.)

3 Hang the border as shown on pages 82–83. If you're lucky, the pattern of the wallpaper itself will give you a level guideline to follow, eliminating the need to make a new pencil guideline.

1 Using a border to separate two different wallpapers can be very effective. Before hanging the wallpaper, make a pencil line on the wall at the height where the center of the border will go. Hang the two papers at the same time with each overlapping the pencil line by 2 inches.

CREATING WALL PANELS WITH A MITERED FRAME

For wall panels, make the first or top measurement equal to the length of the top of the panel. Continue to measure for the other three sides. This will ensure consistency with any other panels you apply. But if you're making just one frame, the top horizontal guideline is all you need.

MITERED FRAME

1 Use a pencil and level to make a horizontal guideline above the window to the width of the finished border. Cut the first length of border 2 inches longer than the length required. Paste the border as shown on pages 82–83 and hang it following the pencil guideline. Make sure that the border overlaps equally on each side of the frame.

2 Cut the first vertical length, again making it 2 inches longer than the height required. Paste it and hang it on the wall using the level to maintain an exact vertical. The overlap is helpful for adjusting the pattern so you can cut through the busiest part of the design (see Step 3), making the joint less visible.

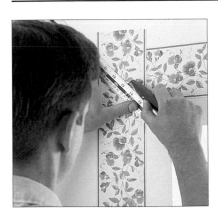

3 Hold a steel rule at a 45-degree angle from the outside to the inside corner of the border frame. Carefully cut through the two lengths of border using a crafts knife.

4 Peel back the two long strips of border, and then remove the excess flaps that are stuck to the wall. Finally, brush the paper back into position creating a mitered joint.

5 Hang the second vertical length of border and, finally, the bottom horizontal length. Use a clean, damp sponge to remove excess adhesive from all the surfaces.

Problems and mistakes

Sometimes after you've finished papering, problems will occur. Some of them are relatively easy to fix, but others may require stripping and rehanging new paper in the problem area. The next four pages illustrate solutions to the most common wallpaper problems.

TOOLS: Bucket, sponge, paper-hanging brush, crafts knife, seam roller, brush

MATERIALS: Water, seam adhesive, felt-tip pen

OVERLAPPING OR LIFTING SEAMS

  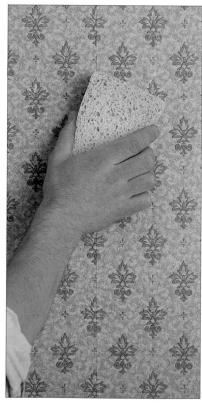

1 Small overlaps can occur when papering, and the paper may not form a strong bond there, especially with vinyl papers. As a result, the edge lifts away from the wall.

2 Use a brush to apply seam adhesive. If the overlap is too small to use a brush, carefully lift the paper away from the wall with the blunt edge of a crafts knife. Then brush on the adhesive.

3 Use a damp sponge to smooth the paper back into position, removing any excess adhesive in the process. Or, use a seam roller to push the paper back down on the wall.

BUBBLING PAPER

1 Determine the cause of the bubbles. Some bubbles in the surface of a wall covering are caused by excess wet paste; these will disappear when the paper dries. You can test for this by gently pressing down on the bubble to feel for the paste. However, when the paper dries completely, any bubbles that remain are the result of trapped air; such bubbles will not disappear on their own. Normally, these are caused by not letting the paper soak long enough before applying the paper to the walls or because the wall surface was poorly prepared.

2 If there are only a few bubbles, pierce each bubble with a crafts knife and use a brush to apply some paste or seam adhesive to the wall. Stick the paper back down and sponge off any excess adhesive.

If the problem is extensive, strip the paper, prepare the wall thoroughly, and next time remember to let the paper soak for the required time before hanging it.

CREASES

Creases are caused by sloppy application or stretching paper around an outside corner that's not square. Repair them as you would bubbling paper. If the problem is extensive, strip and rehang new paper.

WHITE SEAMS

1 White seams usually are the result of two things: One, you or your paper-hanger may have created poor butt joints. Two, the paper may have shrunk while drying. This is especially common in new homes that haven't completely settled. If the problem is severe, you may have to strip the old paper and hang new paper.

2 To avoid white seams, it's always a good idea to let a new house settle for about a year before hanging any wall coverings. To fix a minor problem, use a felt-tip pen or crayon that matches the background color of the paper and carefully run it down the seam. Some paper manufacturers provide special felt-tip pens for this purpose.

Problems and mistakes

Most wallpaper problems occur because of poor application or inadequate surface preparation, rather than defects with the paper itself. Always take your time when hanging wallpaper because some mistakes can be fixed only by stripping the entire area and starting over. This is not only frustrating but expensive.

TOOLS: Bucket, sponge, paper-hanging brush, pasting brush, crafts knife, seam roller

MATERIALS: Water, seam adhesive

WATER STAINS

Before panicking over water stains, let the paper dry out completely. With some heavy papers, this may take several days. If any patches still don't disappear, strip the paper and treat the moisture problem in the wall (see pages 28–29).

SAGGING PAPER

Sagging paper usually is caused by applying too much pressure with the paper-hanging brush, inadvertently stretching and creasing the wet, pliable paper. If the problem is too glaring, you'll need to strip and repaper.

POOR PATTERN MATCH

This problem usually is a result of poor application, in which case the only solution is to strip the paper and start the process over again. Sometimes, however, the pattern fails to match along only a portion of a seam. This is especially common if the paper has been hand-printed. In some cases, the paper may be from a bad lot; always check how well the pattern matches early in the job. (See pages 52, 54–55, and 64–65.)

PASTE ON PAPER OR STAINED SEAMS

If paste dries on the surface of the paper, it can leave a permanent stain (especially on matte-finish wallpapers). This is caused by not wiping wet paste from the surface during paper hanging. If the paper is washable, try removing the paste with a sponge and a mild detergent solution. Similarly, shiny seams can result where joints were over-brushed during application, leaving a polished look. Unfortunately, there's no way to correct this problem.

TORN PAPER

This is caused by accidentally snagging the paper while hanging it. A tear may look irreparable, but by carefully applying seam adhesive and pushing the paper back into place, most tears can be made to look practically invisible.

FLATTENED RELIEF

This is caused by applying too much pressure to embossed papers while hanging the paper. Never use a seam roller on embossed papers. Small areas aren't too noticeable, but large areas may need to be stripped and repapered.

Cleaning up

When the last length of paper is hung, you'll want to spend some time cleaning up. There's nothing worse than finding stiff brushes, grimy buckets, and paste-covered scissors when you start your next papering project.

Storage is important, too. Be sure to seal and store unused adhesives according to the manufacturer's instructions. Also, store any unused rolls of paper in a dry place, and tape opened rolls to prevent them from unrolling and becoming damaged.

TOOLS: Sponge, bucket with lid, nail

MATERIALS: Detergent, clean cloth, water

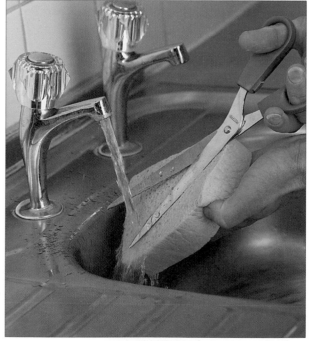

1 Wash the paper-hanging brush under warm running water, using household detergent to remove any dry paste. Rinse thoroughly and allow to dry before storing. To clean the pasting brush, remove as much excess paste from the bristles as you can. Then wash, rinse, and dry in the same way.

2 Rinse the paper-hanging scissors under warm water, taking care to sponge off any dry paste that remains on them; such paste can dull the blades and make future paper-hanging jobs more difficult. To prevent the formation of damaging rust, dry the scissors with a clean cloth.

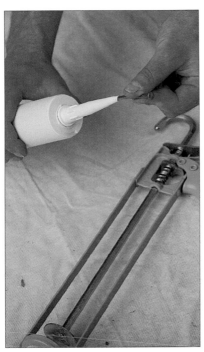

3 If you have leftover paste and might need more in the near future, it can be stored for a few weeks in an airtight container. Read and follow the manufacturer's directions.

4 Wipe the table with clean water and a sponge, focusing especially on edges where paste usually collects. If it's foldable, wait until the table is completely dry before folding and stowing.

5 Follow the manufacturer's instructions and seal a partly used tube of sealant or flexible filler so that it won't dry out. Insert a nail in the end of the nozzle to keep the opening clear.

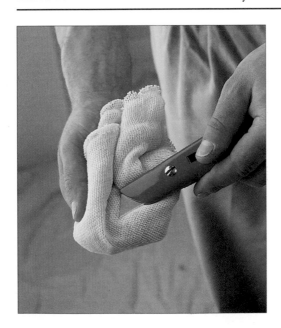

6 Before storing a crafts knife, carefully wipe it clean with a damp cloth to remove all traces of wallpaper paste. Then dry the knife thoroughly and store in a childproof place. For safety's sake, dispose of old blades—they can cause severe cuts even if they seem dull—by placing them inside a sealable container, such as an empty paint can. Make sure that the can is securely sealed before disposing of it. Or, check with local officials and recycle used blades if that is an option in your community.

PASTE DISPOSAL
Most wallpaper paste contains fungicide and isn't biodegradable. Never pour leftover paste down a drain, where it could contribute to water pollution. Instead, dispose of it according to your city's guidelines for handling potentially hazardous materials.

Glossary

Border
A narrow, decorative band of wallpaper.

Butt joint
A joint at which two edges of wallpaper or lining paper meet but don't overlap.

Centering
Placing the dominant part of a wallpaper pattern on a focal point in a room, such as the middle of a fireplace.

Chalk line
A length of string covered in chalk dust, pulled tight, and snapped against a surface to leave a straight guideline.

Double lining
Two layers of lining paper, used to achieve a smooth finish on a rough surface.

Flush
The term used to describe two level, adjacent surfaces.

Fungicide
A chemical that kills mold.

Inside corner
A corner that doesn't protrude into a room.

Lumber
A length of straight wood, used as a guide.

Lining paper
Plain paper that provides a smooth surface on walls and ceilings before painting or hanging wallpaper.

Miter
An angled cut, made when joining two lengths of border to change their direction. It's usually a 45-degree cut that makes a 90-degree corner.

Outside corner
A corner that protrudes into a room.

Overlapping butt joint
The process of overlapping wall coverings, cutting through both layers of paper, and removing the excess strips to create a flush butt joint.

Paste-the-wall paper
Paper applied dry to a wall that has been coated with paste.

Pattern drop
The misalignment of a pattern match.

Pattern repeat
The area over which a pattern repeats itself on a length of wallpaper.

Plumb line
A length of string to which a weight is attached, providing a true vertical guideline.

Prepasted paper
Paper that has been coated with paste during manufacture. The dried paste is reactivated by soaking the paper before hanging.

Recessed window
A window that's flush with an outside wall, creating a recess inside a room.

Seam roller
A small, narrow plastic, felt, or wooden roller used on wallpaper seams to ensure good adhesion.

Size
A stabilizing compound applied to porous surfaces to seal them before hanging wallpaper.

Soaking
Allowing the wallpaper paste to soak into the paper.

Stripping
The removal of old wallpaper from a wall or ceiling.

Tooth
A slightly rough surface that's been sanded to provide a bond for paint or paper.

Trim
Decorative molding around a door or window that covers the joint between the frame and the wall.

Wall-ceiling junction
The line at which a wall meets the ceiling.

Wallpaper trough
A specially shaped container available at wallpaper and paint stores, and designed to hold water for soaking prepasted papers before hanging.

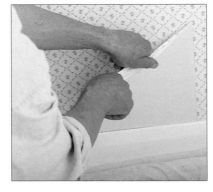

Index

Meredith® Press
An imprint of Meredith® Books

Do-It-Yourself Decorating
Step-by-Step Wallpapering
Editor, Shelter Books: Denise L. Caringer
Contributing Editor: David A. Kirchner
Contributing Designer: Jeff Harrison
Copy Chief: Angela K. Renkoski

Meredith® Books
Editor in Chief: James D. Blume
Managing Editor: Christopher Cavanaugh
Director, New Product Development: Ray Wolf
Vice President, Retail Sales: Jamie L. Martin

Meredith Publishing Group
President, Publishing Group: Christopher M. Little
Vice President and Publishing Director: John P. Loughlin

Meredith Corporation
Chairman of the Board and Chief Executive Officer: Jack D. Rehm
President and Chief Operating Officer: William T. Kerr
Chairman of the Executive Committee: E. T. Meredith III

First published 1996 by Haynes Publishing

All of us at Meredith® Books are dedicated to providing you with information and ideas you need to
enhance your home. We welcome your comments and suggestions about this book on stenciling.
Write to us at: Meredith® Books, Do-It-Yourself Editorial Department,
RW-206, 1716 Locust St., Des Moines, IA 50309-3023.

This edition published by Meredith Corporation, Des Moines Iowa, 1997
Printed in France
Printing Number and Year: 5 4 3 2 1 00 99 98 97 96
Library of Congress Catalog Card Number: 96-78044
ISBN: 0-696-20680-3